The Theory of Capit

How theory meets practice in the German market

Author:
Benjamin Friedrich

FRANKFURTER SCHRIFTEN ZU BANKING AND FINANCE

Herausgegeben von Prof. Dr. Ralf Jasny

ISSN 1861-096X

1   *Werner Winklmann*
     Optionsstrategien in einem Rentenportfolio mit Eurex-Produkten
     ISBN 3-89821-534-2

2   *Benjamin Friedrich*
     The Theory of Capital Structure
     How theory meets practice in the German market
     ISBN 3-89821-539-3

In Vorbereitung:

Christian Fießer
Insolvenzdiagnose anhand von Abschlusskennzahlen von Wachstumsunternehmen
am neuen Markt mit Hilfe des statistischen Verfahrens der logistischen Regression
ISBN 3-89821-541-5

Benjamin Friedrich

THE THEORY OF CAPITAL STRUCTURE

How theory meets practice in the German market

ibidem-Verlag
Stuttgart

Bibliografische Information Der Deutschen Bibliothek

Die Deutsche Bibliothek verzeichnet diese Publikation in der Deutschen Nationalbibliografie; detaillierte bibliografische Daten sind im Internet über <http://dnb.ddb.de> abrufbar.

∞

Gedruckt auf alterungsbeständigem, säurefreien Papier
Printed on acid-free paper

ISSN: 1861-096X

ISBN: 3-89821-539-3

© *ibidem*-Verlag
Stuttgart 2005
Alle Rechte vorbehalten

Printed in Germany

FOREWORD

For years, various theories of capital structure have been the subject of a heated discussion. On the one hand there is the traditional thesis of optimal capital structure, on the other the Modigliani-Miller theory. Although both theories explain the optimal relationship between equity and debt, they do not reconcile and arrive at completely different results and options for action.

This work is an attempt to explore the question of the extent to which these theories have been reflected in the financing behaviour of German firms. To this end, an investigation of the pharmaceutical industry as an example seeks to reveal the extent to which capital structure can throw light on key indicators such as size, growth and profitability. The work is not merely a robust account of the different theories of capital structure, but in addition points to an empirically founded approach which helps to refute the testimony of those theories.

The work is directed not only at students and scientists devoting their efforts to methodological questions of research, but above all to those involved in the practicalities of corporate finance. In this work, the relevance of theories of capital structure to the practice of company financing is illustrated using the example of the German market for the first time.

Prof. Dr. Ralf Jasny

ABSTRACT

This book examines capital structure theory and investigates its practical relevance for the German market using exemplary data from the pharmaceutical and healthcare industry. The main objectives of this analysis are to explore the link between capital structure theory and corporate practice and to test determinants of capital structure choice empirically. It starts with an examination of capital structure theories and introduces the most important theoretical models that have been advanced to explain corporate debt policy in practice. Next, it examines existing empirical evidence on capital structure theories and introduces theoretical proxies of determinants of capital structure which can be used to investigate the financing behaviour of companies statistically. Thereafter, it introduces a multiple regression model to investigate the practical relevance of capital structure theories for the German pharmaceutical and healthcare industry. Finally, it uses the results of the statistical analysis to estimate the optimal level of debt for one pharmaceutical company and illustrates how the company might benefit from moving closer to its optimum debt level using the cost of capital approach. Major findings of the analysis are that leverage is highly influenced by growth opportunities and firm size and that the introduced regression model is adequate to estimate the optimal level of debt for an individual firm in line with the assumed industry optimum.[*]

---

[*] I like to thank Ursula Kockerbeck, Eva Wycisk and Debbie Lindsay for their helpful comments regarding the intricacies of the English language during the revision process. I also like to thank Ralf Jasny (the editor) and Commerzbank Securities DCM and CMAD for their support making the empirical investigation possible. Above all I thank my parents for their longstanding and ongoing support during my under- and postgraduate studies.

LIST OF ABBREVATIONS

[Amer.]	–	American English
[Brit.]	–	British English
BP	–	Breusch-Pagan
CAPM	–	Capital Asset Pricing Model
CFO	–	Chief Financial Officer
chap.	–	Chapter
et al.	–	And others (et alii)
e.g.	–	For example (exempli gratia)
EU	–	European Union
GAAP	–	Generally Accepted Accounting Principles
GNP	–	Gross National Product
GROPP	–	Growth opportunities
G-7	–	Germany, France, Italy Japan, United States, United Kingdom and Canada
HGB	–	Handelsgesetzbuch (German GAAP)
IFRS	–	International Financial Reporting Standards
i.e.	–	That is (id est)
LEV	–	Leverage
LM	–	Lagrange Multiplier
M&M	–	Modigliani and Miller
NDTS	–	Non debt tax shields
NPV	–	Net Present Value
PROF	–	Profitability
PV	–	Present Value
P&H	–	Pharmaceutical and Healthcare
R&D	–	Research and Development
TANG	–	Tangibility
US	–	United States
VOL	–	Volatility
vs.	–	Against (versus)
WACC	–	Weighted Average Cost of Capital

$C_1 = \overline{X_j}$	–	Expected future cash flow/ income
g	–	Growth rate
i_j	–	Expected rate of return on equity
K_d	–	Cost of debt before tax
K_e	–	Risk adjusted cost of equity
$K_0 = K_u$	–	Weighted Average Cost of Capital
r_d	–	Interest rate for debt
$R_f = r$	–	Risk free rate of return
$\overline{R_j} = i_j$	–	Required rate of return on equity
$\overline{R_m}$	–	Average or index return on the market
t_c	–	Corporate tax rate
t_{pd}	–	Personal income tax rate for debt
t_{ps}	–	Personal income tax rate for equity of the firm's assets
$V_d = D_j$	–	Market values of a firm's debt
$V_d\, t_c$	–	Present value of its interest tax shields on debt
$V_e = S_j$	–	Market values of a firm's equity
V_g	–	Market value of a levered firm
V_j	–	Market value of the firm
V_u	–	Market value of an all-equity financed firm
β_j	–	Company risk in relation to the market risk
ρ_k	–	Discount rate appropriate to the risk class

LIST OF FIGURES AND TABLES

CONTENTS

1 Introduction

1.1 About the existence of an optimal capital structure

The theory of capital structure is one of the most exciting and complex topics in corporate finance. After many years of debate it is still extremely difficult to provide a conclusive answer to the questions of which capital structure maximises the value of a firm and what factors determine the optimal mix of debt and equity capital. Ideally, optimal capital structure maximizes shareholder value, maintains an adequate level of liquidity, ensures financial flexibility and maintains a tolerable level of financial risk (Williamson and Francis, 2001). Even if these goals are complementary and ensuring liquidity at all times should be the overriding principle, they are to some extent in conflict and large amounts of cash or reserves may be preferred by bondholders and managers although they represent an opportunity loss for shareholders.

Most frequently, optimal capital structure is defined as the optimal proportion of debt and equity that maximizes the value of the firm. This is the objective in most commercial organisations as it maximizes shareholder wealth and increases the competitiveness of the firm (Arnold, 2002). Even if optimal capital structure is geared to only one theoretical objective, financial theorists have not yet identified the universal rules that optimize capital structure for any given firm at any given time. This is due, to some extent, on conflicts between the existing theories and the difficulty in designing a meaningful empirical test that explains corporate financing behaviour adequately. Nevertheless, comprehensive knowledge about capital structure theory and empirical evidence of corporate practice enhances the process of managing and optimizing capital structure and it is therefore useful to identify firm specific or industry related factors that drive companies towards their optimum.

The Theory of Capital Structure

The modern theory of capital structure began with the celebrated paper of Franco Modigliani and Merton Miller (1958). Their propositions show that the value of a firm is independent of its capital structure and depends primarily on the firm's investment strategy and future earnings potential. Before 1958 most financial theorists believed that the value of a firm could be maximised by increasing its level of debt. This is based on the fact that debt is a cheaper source of financing and interest payouts are tax deducible, whereas equity is more expensive and dividends are paid out after tax. From this point, the great debate between the so-called traditionalists and the supporters of Modigliani and Miller began.

In the early 1960s, Modigliani and Miller modified their conclusion by including corporate tax in their model of capital structure and showed that an optimal capital structure does, in fact, exist and that it can be found exactly at the point where the level of debt is at its maximum. However, this conclusion, as well as their earlier propositions, are based on some unrealistic assumptions about the real world and empirical evidence of corporate practice shows that fully debt or equity financed companies rarely exist. In 1966 Robichek and Myers pointed out that optimizing capital structure involves a balancing of tax advantage and bankruptcy costs. Accordingly, the optimal capital structure that maximises the value of a firm would be exactly where the marginal advantage of debt is offset by the marginal disadvantage of bankruptcy costs (Bradley et al, 1984). This view was criticised when Merton Miller (1977) presented a new model of capital structure irrelevancy and demonstrated that the tax advantage of debt on the corporate level is exactly offset by the income tax disadvantage on the personal level. Although Millers model is based on some unrealistic assumptions, it shows that the gain of leverage is much smaller than previously thought and that an optimal capital structure exists for the corporate sector as a whole, rather than for an individual firm. Over the years, additional theories and capital market imperfections supporting the relevance of capital structure evolved, such as the objective of minimizing agency costs (Jensen and Meckling, 1976), the preference of managers to issue debt as a positive signal for future earnings potential (Ross, 1977) or the pecking order theory (Myers, 1984; Myers and Majluf, 1984). The latter argues that companies have no target capital structure and prefer to finance in accordance with their cost of financing, starting with internally generated funds, over debt to external equity (Clark, 1993).

1.2   Aims of the book and methodology

This book examines the practical relevance of capital structure theory and discusses its importance for the German market. The main objectives of this analysis are to explore the link between capital structure theory and corporate practice and to provide empirical evidence of determinants of capital structure choice, using cross sectional, firm specific data from the German pharmaceutical and healthcare (P&H) industry.

The first part of this book focuses on the theory of optimal capital structure. It starts with a review of financial theory and introduces some important concepts that have been advanced to explain the relationship between capital structure, average cost of capital and firm value. Next, it discusses alternative views on capital structure theory, including the traditional approach and the Modigliani and Miller (M&M) theory. After that, it investigates the impact of taxes, financial distress and agency costs and explains how these market imperfections may determine optimal capital structure. In addition, this part covers models based on asymmetric information, signalling and the pecking order theory. Emphasis will be on the explanation and critical appraisal of important capital structure theories without attempting to offer mathematical proof or further in depth investigation. Additional financial concepts related to the capital structure debate, for example equity valuation models or the capital asset pricing model (CAPM) are introduced and taken at face value without further discussion or criticism. The discussion of related topics on capital structure theory, such as investment appraisal, dividend policy, alternative types of debt and equity instruments or the maturity structure of debt, is not within the scope of this investigation.

Secondly, this book surveys existing empirical evidence on capital structure theory and assesses the relevance of the theoretical models in explaining corporate financing behaviour in practice. In particular, it focuses on two main competing theories: the strategic trade-off and the pecking order theory. Furthermore it introduces explanatory factors of leverage that are likely to affect the firm's capital structure choice in practice. It starts by surveying some important and recent empirical evidence of the trade-off theory including evidence on industry and target leverage ratios, taxes and financial distress and continues with empirical evidence of the pecking order theory including asymmetric information and signalling. The analysis focuses particularly on cross sectional studies using statistical modelling techniques, including linear regression and structural equation modelling as well as empirical surveys based on data mainly from the United States and Europe. The main emphasis is on a brief discussion of the empirical results and their relation to theory. Due to the limited scope of this work, the empirical results of the introduced studies are taken at face value and the experimental design of the studies are not discussed or criticised. Additionally, this part summarizes theoretical proxies of determinants of capital structure which have been advanced by capital structure theories and have been used in previous empirical studies. For ease of comparison with previous empirical work this part includes a brief discussion of important institutional settings in Germany.

The third part of the book investigates the practical relevance of capital structure theories and empirical evidence of corporate practice for the German market using exemplary data from the P&H industry. It investigates the existence of an optimal capital structure at an industry and firm level by analysing determinants of capital structure choice by using a linear regression model and applying the cost of capital approach to Schwarz Pharma

AG. The regression analysis investigates determinants of capital structure choice by examining the linear relationship between leverage and six explanatory variables, including SIZE, TANGIBILITY, GROWTH, PROFITABILITY, VOLATILITY AND NON-DEBT-TAXSHIELDS. The analysis focuses thereby on quantitatively oriented questions of corporate leverage and investigates the relationship between theoretical attributes and empirical proxies based on certain accounting indicators. The cost of capital approach investigates Schwartz Pharma AG's weighted average cost of capital, its cost of equity and cost of debt and uses the results of the previously investigated regression model to determine a theoretically optimal level of debt in capital structure.

Despite its limitations, the study makes three significant contributions to literature. Firstly, most of the capital structure theories have been tested in the US and within an international context. To what extent these theories are applicable to a particular industry in the German market has not been explored. Secondly, the analysis highlights the importance of two company specific factors which particularly influence the leverage decision of firms within the German P&H industry – the proxies for size and growth opportunities. Thirdly, the application of a regression model to identify an industry optimum in combination with the cost of capital approach in order to estimate the theoretical optimum for an individual firm is new and even if this approach is based on several assumptions, the empirical investigation of the P&H industry has shown that it is adequate to identify a target range of optimal capital structure in correspondence with the sample data and the assumed industry optimum.

2 Theoretical foundations

The identification of an optimal capital structure is one of the most complex and challenging tasks in corporate finance. Most frequently, optimizing capital structure is equated with the objective of maximising the market value of a firm and shareholder wealth. The discounted cash flow model in the theory of enterprise valuation postulates that the market value of a firm depends on the sum of its future earnings potential, discounted to its present value (Arnold, 2002).

$$(1) \qquad V_j = \frac{C_1}{WACC}$$

(*Source: Arnold, 2002 p.814)

Assuming a perpetual cash flow stream (i.e. no growth), efficient stock markets and a constant discount rate, the value of the firm (V_j), which should be equal to the market value of the firms debt and equity capital, would be a function of the future cash flows (C_1) and the weighted average cost of capital (WACC). In this connexion it is obvious that the market value of a firm could be enhanced by either increasing its future earnings potential or decreasing the firm's overall cost of capital. The latter (WACC) is a function of risk and return and is calculated by multiplying the weighted proportions of debt and equity capital with the risk-adjusted rates of return.[1]

$$(2) \qquad K_0 = K_e \frac{V_e}{V_e + V_d} + K_d (1 - t_c) \frac{V_d}{V_e + V_d}$$

(*Source: Samuels et al, 1996 p.648)

---

[1] K_0= WACC, K_e = risk adjusted cost of equity, K_d = cost of debt before tax, V_e = market value of equity, V_d = market value of debt, t_c = corporate tax rate, $K_d (1 - t_c)$ = the after-tax cost of debt. The extension of the formula by distinguishing between common and preferred stock share capital is renounced.

The WACC (K_0) is the overall cost of debt and equity capital and represents the minimum return required for an investment project in order to guarantee a satisfactory return for investors. Assuming the validity of these theories, as well as efficient stock markets, the value of ordinary shares should be maximised where the overall cost of capital is minimized. Therefore, the objective of minimising the cost of capital equals the goal of maximising the value of the firm and shareholder wealth.

The risk-adjusted rate of return for debt (K_e) and equity (K_d) depends thereby on the company's overall level of risk, which can be split into business and financial risk. Business risk is related to the operations of a firm and is influenced by company specific factors, such as industry or market risk. Financial risk is related to the financial policy of a firm and depends on the proportion of debt to equity in capital structure. It is frequently measured by the financial leverage [Amer.] or gearing [Brit.] ratio, which could be defined as the book value of long term debt to shareholder funds (Arnold, 2002).

The advantage of debt over equity financing is based on the fact that debt is generally a cheaper source of financing than equity. Furthermore debt carries less risk than equity because maturity dates and interest payments are usually fixed and debt holders have prior claims on the annual income and the residual value of the firm's assets in the case of liquidation. In addition, a company pays effectively less for debt than for equity, because transaction costs of raising and servicing debt are generally lower and interest charges are tax deducible, whereas dividends are paid out after tax. Besides these facts, equity capital has a higher level of risk because shareholders' claims are based on the firm's residual income and residual value in the case of liquidation. In comparison to debt, it is a more secure source of funding and the company has no obligation to pay dividends or to repay the capital. In summary, the main disadvantages of equity are its high issuing and servicing costs and the fact that dividends are not tax deductible. However debt is only cheaper than equity because there is an equity base that takes the risk and excessive borrowing always increases the risk of financial distress for both debt holders and shareholders (Arnold, 2002).

Risk and return considerations are also the reasons why shareholders are motivated to accept a higher level of risk. The capital structure debate is partly concerned with the trade-off between risk and return and the benefits of debt over equity financing.

The cost of equity or the minimum required rate of return that a company must earn to satisfy its shareholders can be calculated in terms of a factor model using multiple risk components or a single risk component, as the level of systematic risk[2] (β_j) in the capital asset pricing model (Van Horne, 1998). The CAPM relates the required rate of return for equity capital ($\overline{R}_j$) to the company's level of systematic risk (β_j) and the average- ($\overline{R}_m$) and risk-free (R_f) rate of return in the market.

$$(3) \qquad \overline{R}_j = R_f + (\overline{R}_m - R_f) * \beta_j$$

(*Source: Van Horne, 1998 p.68)

The expected return on an investment for a given level of systematic risk results from the return on the risk free rate (R_f), plus the excess return on the market portfolio ($\overline{R}_m - R_f$), multiplied by the company's individual level of systematic risk (β_j)[3]. The greater the systematic risk of an investment opportunity, the greater the expected rate of return will be for the investor.

---

[2] Systematic risk is the company's unavoidable exposure to market wide factors, which is common to all firms and cannot be diversified away.
[3] The beta factor (β) simply measures the sensitivity of a security excess return on a particular share with the market portfolio as a whole.

3   The theory of capital structure and the value of the firm

3.1   Traditional view of capital structure theory

The examination of alternative theories of capital structure begins with the traditional view, which assumes that a firm can maximise its market value through the optimal level of gearing. As previously outlined, the traditional approach uses the WACC to illustrate how the market value of a firm can be maximised by minimising the average cost of capital.

FIGURE 1:

Traditional approach to capital structure theory

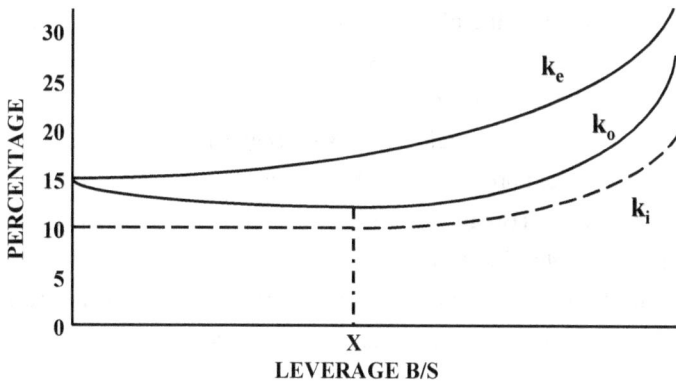

(Own illustration; based on: Van Horne, 1998 p.255)

The traditional approach assumes that moderate levels of debt do not significantly add to the risk of holding debt, but any increase in leverage increases the required rate of return on equity. The above shown variation of the traditional approach illustrates that the weighted average cost of capital (k_0) initially declines as the level of debt in capital structure increases. After a certain point, the advantage of using lower cost debt is exactly offset by the higher required rate of return for equity (k_e) and the WACC is at its minimum. As the level of debt continues to increase, debt holders start to require a higher rate of return for debt (k_d) and the WACC starts to rise at an increasing rate. The optimal level of gearing would now be exactly at point X, where the weighted average cost of capital (k_0) is at its lowest and any additional gain from using "*cheaper*" debt is exactly offset by the higher required rate of return for debt (Van Horne, 1998).

The traditional approach assumes that the market value of a firm is maximised when the WACC is minimised and any additional benefit of debt is offset by the higher required return for equity. However, minimising the WACC is not necessarily equivalent to the objective of maximising the value of the firm. If future cash flows are positively affected by the tax advantage provided by debt, the value of a firm could also be enhanced by increasing the present value of the interest tax shield. Accordingly, the optimal capital structure that maximises the value of a firm can differ from the capital structure that minimises the WACC. The optimal level of debt could now be determined by the gain from using cheaper debt and the gain from the interest tax shield provided by debt in relation to the higher required rate of return for equity (Brealey and Myers, 1996). However, tax shields are only beneficial if the firm has taxable income, otherwise there would be no tax benefits from using debt. Furthermore, if tax-loss carry forwards are possible, the present value of the tax shield would be less significant and decline through the opportunity loss of the immediate outflow and the postponed capitalization of the tax benefits.

Another substantial critique of the traditional approach is the assumed relationship between risk and return. The traditional view assumes that a moderate level of gearing does not affect the cost of debt. Given that higher levels of debt increase the risk for both equity and debt holders, the one-side adjustment on equity return leads to an opportunity loss for debt holders. In addition, debt holders bear a higher proportion of the overall risk and transfer some of their wealth to shareholders. This lowers the overall risk for shareholders and should theoretically lead to a lower required rate of return on equity capital (Bitz, 2000). Furthermore, new borrowings may increase the risk of senior debt and in the case that the rate of return is only adjusted for new borrowings, old debt holders would experience an opportunity loss and shift some of their wealth to the providers of the new debt capital. On the other hand, if the benefits of debt are exactly offset by the higher expected rate of return on equity, the WACC would be constant and the value of the firm would be independent from its leverage decision. This and some additional arguments will be investigated more thoroughly in the following section.

3.2 Capital structure irrelevance in perfect capital markets

3.2.1 Independence of capital structure and firm value

In their 1958 paper, *"The Cost of Capital, Corporation Finance and the Theory of Investment"*, Franco Modigliani and Merton Miller show that under a certain set of assumptions, the financing decision of a firm does not affect the firm's value or its cost of capital. Even though most financial theorists nowadays believe that capital structure does affect the value of the firm, it is important to understand the conditions under which capital structure is irrelevant, in order to fully understand why capital structure matters and which market imperfections make one capital structure better than another (Brealey and Myers, 1996). According to their theoretical model, M&M conclude that the WACC is not affected by financial leverage and the only factor that affects the value of a firm is its future earnings potential. Thus, the value of a firm and shareholder wealth can only be enhanced by good investment decisions and not by financial policy. Given that the assumptions under which the M&M propositions apply are important, they are summarized as follows:[4]

---

[4] Note that these propositions are not the original assumptions presented by M&M; they are based on a simpler version presented in Fama (1978) but are as good as the originals.

Assumption 1: *Capital markets are perfect.* There are no transaction costs for agents (investors and firms) and securities are perfectly divisible. There are no contracting costs of bankruptcy or financial distress[5] and no corporate and personal taxes.

Assumption 2: *Equal Access.* Investors can borrow or lend money and issue securities on the same terms and conditions as firms.

Assumption 3: *Homogeneous Expectations.* Information is without cost and available to all agents inside and outside the firm. Firms can be classified into distinct risk and return classes and the future prospects of a firm or a security are correctly assessed.

Assumption 4: *Only wealth counts.* Investors and managers are risk averse wealth maximiser and risk-free arbitrage opportunities are exploited.

Assumption 5: *Given Investment Strategies.* All current and future investment decisions of a firm are presumed to be given and not affected by the financing decision.

M&M show that under these assumptions the value of a firm, its cost of capital and its investment decision are independent from its capital structure. Their conclusions are expressed in form of three propositions.

The first proposition states that *"the market value of any firm is independent of its capital structure and is given by capitalizing its expected return at the rate (ρ_k) appropriate to its risk class"* (Modigliani and Miller, 1958 p. 268); their original notation stated this as

$$(4) \qquad V_j = S_j + D_j = \frac{\overline{X}_j}{\rho_k}$$

(*Source: Culp, 2003 p.81)

---

[5] Assets can be sold at their economic values and there are no legal or administrative costs.

The total market value of a firm (V_j), which equals the market values of its equity (S_j) and debt (D_j), is the net present value of the expected income stream $(\overline{X}_j)$ at the discount rate appropriate to the risk class of the firm's assets (ρ_k). The WACC (ρ_k) is assumed to be independent from the leverage decision and the value of the firm is therefore independent from changes in capital structure (Culp, 2003).

Proposition one is based on the idea that investors are able to manufacture *"home made leverage"* by substituting personal for corporate debt and are thereby able to replicate the capital structure of any firm by themselves (Van Horne, 1998). Two identical firms with the same assets and investment opportunities should consequently yield the same payoff and should also have the same market value, even if their capital structures are different. If their market values are unequal, investors would be able to achieve a risk-free arbitrage by moving from the overvalued to the undervalued company, adjusting their leverage by themselves and maintaining the same level of financial risk. This process would continue until the two firms are at equilibrium, selling at the same price in the market (Samuels et al, 1996). As a result of this arbitrage, the market value of two similar firms should be equal and independent of their capital structure decisions.

3.2.2   Financial leverage and the weighted average cost of capital

M&M's second proposition states that *"the expected rate of return on equity increases linearly with the debt to equity ratio"*; mathematically this can be expressed as

$$(5) \qquad i_j = \rho_k + (\rho_k - r) * \frac{D_j}{S_j}$$

(*Source: Culp, 2003 p.83)

15

Equation (5) postulates that the expected rate of return on equity (i_j) equals the expected return on a pure equity stream (ρ_k) plus a premium for financial risk, expressed by debt ratio in capital structure ($\frac{D_j}{S_j}$), times the excess return between the expected rate of return on a pure equity stream (ρ_k) and the expected return on debt (r). This proposition shows that the benefits from using "*cheaper*" debt are exactly offset by the higher expected rate of return on equity, leading to a constant WACC, irrespective of the level of debt in capital structure (Culp, 2003).

Proposition two is simply illustrated by rearranging the WACC formula (4) already introduced above, adjusted to the assumption of perfect capital markets and no corporate taxes.[6]

$$(6) \qquad K_e = K_u + \frac{V_d}{V_e}(K_u - K_d)$$

(*Source: Samuels et al, 1996 p.652)

Equation (6) illustrates the independence of firm value and capital structure and is consistent with equation (5) which proposes a linear relationship between the cost of equity and the level of gearing.

3.2.3 Independence of financing and investment decision

Proposition three states that the cut-off rate of return for new investments is equal to the rate of return of a pure equity financed firm (ρ_k) and will be

---

[6]
$$K_0 = K_u = K_e \frac{V_e}{V_e + V_d} + K_d \frac{V_d}{V_e + V_d} \quad \text{(Multiplied by } V_e + V_d)$$

$$K_u V_e + K_u V_d = V_e K_e + V_d K_d \quad \text{(Divided by } V_e \text{ and solved to } K_e)$$

$$K_e = K_u + \frac{V_d}{V_e}(K_u - K_d)$$

constant regardless of the firm's capital structure choice (Arnold, 2002). This is already proven by proposition two, which shows that the WACC is constant and equal to the cost of equity of an all-equity financed firm. All three propositions are therefore consistent with and related to proposition one as well as the idea of arbitrage discussed above.

Most of the critiques of M&M's theory are based on the implausibility of their assumptions. The question that arises on the arbitrage argument is whether personal investors are able to replicate capital structure and borrow on the same terms and conditions as firms do. This criticism can partly be offset by the argument that arbitrage can also be carried out by intermediaries acting on behalf of investors, such as investment banks, which are able to secure the same terms and conditions as firms (Culp, 2003). In addition, there are various reasons for suspecting that personal and corporate leverage are perfect substitutes. Firstly, personal borrowing is more likely to be more expensive than corporate borrowing. Secondly, personal borrowing may have certain drawbacks for investors, such as the unlimited liability for personal loans, whereas stockholders have limited liability. Thirdly, many institutional investors, such as pension funds or insurance companies, have regulatory restrictions on their investment behaviour and are not allowed to engage in "*home made leverage*" or to participate in the kind of excessive borrowing described above (Van Horne, 1998). With these personal and institutional restrictions, the arbitrage argument of M&M becomes less significant. One of the most significant differences between reality and the assumptions of M&M are that taxes, transaction- and bankruptcy costs exist and they have to be considered in financial management. However, the M&M theory and the conditions under which their model holds true are a good starting point to identify real world imperfections that may affect the cost of capital and the value of a firm and make capital structure decision relevant.

3.3 The value of the firm with taxes and financial distress

3.3.1 Taxes and capital structure

In their initial model, M&M (1958) demonstrate that the capital structure decision rarely matters in perfect capital markets. As criticised above, their irrelevancy theorem is based on some unrealistic assumptions and is therefore not accepted as a practical guideline in corporate finance. Furthermore, leverage ratios across industries indicate that the capital structure decision is not irrelevant since debt ratios do not vary randomly and many capital intensive industries, such as steel or chemicals rely heavily on debt, whereas start-up or technology companies are predominantly financed with equity (Brealey and Myers, 1996). Consequently, M&M must have ignored some important aspects that make capital structure relevant. The most important market imperfections that may affect the capital structure decision in practice are personal and corporate taxes, as well as financial distress and bankruptcy costs. The following section introduces these aspects and incorporates their impact on firm value into the model of capital structure.

The advantage of debt financing, assuming perfect capital markets and corporate taxes only, relies on the fact that interest payments are tax deductible, but not dividends or retained earnings. More debt in capital structure consequently lowers future tax liabilities and increases the amount of after tax cash flows available to shareholders.

In their 1963 version of the model, M&M made this correction on corporate income tax and demonstrate that the value of the firm can be increased by the present value of the savings related to the firm's income tax liabilities (Clark, 1993). The market value of a leveraged firm (V_g) is consequently equal to the value of an all-equity financed firm (V_u), plus the present value of its interest tax shields on debt $(V_d t_c)$[7].

$$(7) \qquad V_g = V_u + V_d t_c$$

(*Source: Samuels et al, 1996 p.652)

The result suggests that an optimal capital structure that maximises the value of the firm exists and is exactly where the level of debt is at its maximum (assuming risk free debt).

However, the model assumes that the tax savings related to the tax deducibility of interest on debt can always be capitalized. If a firm has low or negative taxable income, these tax benefits would be reduced or even eliminated. In addition, other tax shields such as leasing, depreciation or foreign tax shelters may use up the taxable income beforehand and the benefits of the interest tax shields may be lost when leverage becomes too high (Van Horne, 1998). As a result, the value of a firm increases less than the tax advantage of leverage suggests by itself. Despite the uncertainty that some value of the tax shield remains unused, a firm might also incur other costs such as bankruptcy or financial distress which may offset some of the tax advantages of debt. However, the present value of the interest tax shield on debt might be overstated when considering only corporate taxes and the aim of maximising shareholder wealth may change when personal taxes are also considered.

Introducing personal income tax into the model of capital structure refutes the conclusion that debt is a cheaper and more favourable source of financing than equity. Investors are concerned about their personal income after

---

[7] The present value of the tax shield is calculated by $\dfrac{(V_d t_c) r_d}{r_d} = V_d t_c$. Note that the level of debt is assumed to be constant and the present value factor (r_d) equals the interest rate for debt.

tax. Since many investors receive income from both equity and debt, firms should be primarily concerned with maximising the after tax return of their investors. A higher level of debt lowers the firm's corporate taxes but increases the personal taxes paid by investors. This is because returns paid out as dividends are taxed twice, on a corporate and personal level, whereas interest payments are tax deductible and taxed only once. The present value of the corporate tax shield could now be shown as

$$(8) \text{ Value of tax shield on debt} = V_d\left[1 - \frac{(1-t_c)(1-t_{ps})}{(1-t_{pd})}\right]$$

(*Source: Samuels et al, 1996 p.656)

As before, (V_d) and (t_c) are the market value and the corporate tax rate of the firm's debt, and, (t_{ps}) and (t_{pd}) are the personal income tax rates for equity and debt. The advantage of debt in capital structure now depends on the relevant corporate and personal tax regulations, as well as on the differential between personal and corporate tax rates.

If it is assumed that the return on equity is realized entirely in the form of dividends (it could also be in the form of capital gains) and the personal tax rates on debt and equity are equal (i.e. $t_{ps} = t_{pd}$), the two terms would cancel each other out and the present value of the tax shield becomes $(V_dt_c)^8$, exactly as M&M demonstrate in the corrected version of their model of capital structure. In practice, the effective tax rates on debt and equity income are likely to be different.

As noted above, interest charges on corporate debt are generally tax deductible and provide a tax advantage to firms. Dividends on the other hand are taxed twice at the corporate and personal level. The capital income which investors receive in the form of dividends and interest payouts is

---

[8] Present value of the tax shield = $V_d(1-(1-t_c)) = V_dt_c$.

generally taxed at the same personal tax rates, which ranges from approximately 22% up to 56%[9] in Germany (Rutterford, 1988). Furthermore, the imputation system mitigates for the double taxation of dividends by providing stockholders with credit for taxes already paid by the firm on distributed income. In addition, equity returns in the form of capital gains are also taxed at the investor's personal rate of income, but are only taxable if they exceed an annual exemption limit; otherwise they are tax free (Samuels et al, 1996). Thus capital income from equity tends to be considerably lower than debt, especially if firms have high capital gains and low dividend payout ratios.[10]

The result shows that corporate tax rules subsidize debt, but personal tax rules favour equity. However, the advantage of debt over equity financing depends not only on corporate and personal income tax regulations, but also on a firm's investment and dividend policy. Companies with low dividend payout ratios and consequently higher capital gains are more likely to experience equity as a more favourable source of financing than companies with high dividend payout ratios. In general, these factors suggest that equity is superior to debt financing, but empirical evidence of corporate practice shows that debt financing dominates in Germany (Rutterford, 1988). Therefore, there must be other factors that affect the firm's capital structure decision in practice.

In 1977 Merton Miller proposed a model of optimal capital structure which shows that the irrelevancy of capital structure also holds when both corporate and personal taxes are considered. He suggests that when debt and stock markets are in equilibrium, personal and corporate tax effects would

---

[9] The highest income tax rate of 53% plus the solidarity tax contribution of 5.5% which results in an effective maximum tax rate of approximately 56% (0.53*0.055 ≈ 56%), based on the German tax system in 2002 [see e.g. Bauer (1998) p. 92].

[10] Note that it is not within the scope of this work to discuss the relevant tax regulations for interest, dividend and equity income on the corporate and personal level in detail. The short and consequently inaccurate illustration should introduce major characteristics of regulations, based on the German tax system in 2002.

cancel each other out and changes in capital structure would have no effect on the market value of the firm.

Miller's model assumes that all equity income is received in the form of un-realized capital gains and the personal tax rate on stock income equals zero ($t_{ps} = 0$). The value of the interest tax shield on debt could now be expressed as

$$(9) \text{ Value of the tax shield on debt} = V_d \left[1 - \frac{(1-t_c)}{(1-t_{pd})} \right]$$

(*Source: Samuels et al, 1996 p.657)

Equation (9) shows that the present value of the interest tax shield on debt would be at its maximum when the personal income tax rate for debt (t_{pd}) equals one. In this context, Miller assumes that firms would initially finance their activities entirely with equity. Due to the existence of interest tax shields on debt, managers would prefer to issue some debt in order to in-crease the value of the firm. As the companies begin to borrow, they would try to alter their capital structures in line with the personal tax differential of investors in order to take advantage of low income tax brackets first. Ini-tially, the companies would target tax-exempt investors like pension funds, until their demand for debt is satisfied. As the companies borrow more, they need to persuade investors in higher tax brackets to take their debt. There-fore they have to offer higher rates of return in order to persuade investors to keep their debt and to compensate for any extra tax they have to pay. This process continues until the marginal tax rate of the clientele investing in debt (t_{pd}) equals the corporate tax rate (t_c) and the market of debt and stock are in equilibrium (Van Horne, 1998). Since the benefits of borrowing are exactly offset by the higher required rate of return, any changes in capital structure have no affect on the value of the firm.

In such equilibrium the optimal level of gearing is determined by corporate and personal tax rates, the various tax brackets of different investors and the amount of funds available for investment. If corporate tax rates increase, the new equilibrium would be higher and if personal tax rates increase the optimal level of gearing would be lower. Consequently, it is obvious that this equilibrium is determined by the corporate sector as a whole and cannot be changed by a single firm. Accordingly, Miller suggests that an optimal capital structure does not exist for an individual firm alone, but rather for the corporate sector as a whole.

However, Millers model is only plausible if the personal tax rate on equity income is substantially lower than the personal tax rate on interest income. In practice, companies do pay dividends and investors also realize taxable capital gains and the assumption of zero personal tax rates on equity income does not hold true. Furthermore, Millers' model assumes that all firms have approximately the same marginal tax rate. This assumption can immediately be rejected since the marginal tax rate of many firms is affected by non-debt tax shields such as depreciation, investment tax credits or loss carry forwards and marginal tax rates differ significantly between firms and industries. Nevertheless, Millers' model leads to a better understanding of how personal and corporate taxes affect capital structure and provides some insights into the tax preferences of investors. The general view of most financial managers and economists is that the benefits of using debt are not entirely offset by the opposite tax effects on the personal level and that there is a tax advantage related to corporate borrowing. In addition, Miller himself notes that debt policies are not irrelevant considering all the circumstances of the real world. His model provides the theoretical arguments under which debt policies would still be irrelevant, despite the tax advantage related to debt (Damodaran, 2001).

3.3.2   Capital structure and financial distress

A major disadvantage for firms who wish to take up large amounts of debt is that it increases the level of financial risk and exposes the firm to a higher probability of financial distress. Financial distress occurs when a firm cannot meet its obligations to debt holders or even when it has difficulties to do so (Arnold, 2002). This may lead to bankruptcy and sometimes ultimately to liquidation. The risk associated with financial distress is costly and has a negative affect on firm value. It offsets some value of the interest tax shield on debt and the present value of a firm can be written as:

$$
\begin{array}{c}
\textbf{Present Value} \\
\textbf{(PV) of a firm}
\end{array}
=
\begin{array}{c}
\textbf{Value of an all} \\
\textbf{equity financed} \\
\textbf{firm}
\end{array}
+
\begin{array}{c}
\textbf{PV of} \\
\textbf{tax shield} \\
\textbf{on debt}
\end{array}
-
\begin{array}{c}
\textbf{PV of costs} \\
\textbf{of financial} \\
\textbf{distress}
\end{array}
$$

(*Source: Brealey and Myers, 1996)

The expected costs of financial distress are thereby determined by the costs associated with bankruptcy and the probability of its occurrence. Over a moderate level of gearing these costs are relatively small. But with higher levels of gearing, the probability of financial distress and the required rate of return increases for both shareholders and debt holders. The costs of financial distress, bankruptcy and ultimately liquidation can be divided into direct and indirect costs. The direct costs of financial distress depend on the legal and administrative procedure of bankruptcy and include expenses such as the costs of lawyers and accountants, court fees and management time (Samuels et al, 1996). The indirect costs associated with financial distress are often much greater than the more obvious direct costs and are derived from lost relationships with suppliers, customers and employees and include aspects such as lost sales or lost goodwill. One of the most important indirect costs of bankruptcy is the reduction in firm value through passing up valuable investment projects and lost shareholder value in the case of liquidation. The presence of these costs related to bankruptcy and liquidation increase risk and consequently the required rate of return for both debt and equity capital.

FIGURE 2:
Value of firm with taxes and bankruptcy costs

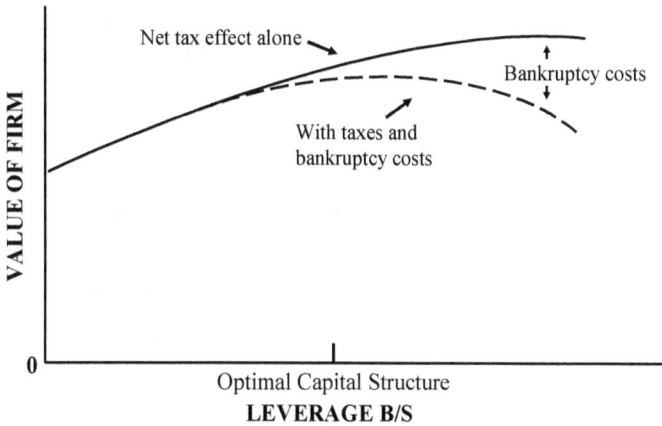

(Own illustration; based on: Van Horne, 1998 p.268)

The advocates of the importance of bankruptcy costs argue that, over a moderate level of gearing, the tax advantage of debt is almost unaffected by the probability of bankruptcy. As the level of debt increases, the probability of financial distress gradually becomes more and more important and the tax advantage of debt is increasingly offset by the higher required rate of return for debt and equity capital as compensation for the increased probability of bankruptcy. After a certain point, these costs exceed the benefits of debt and the value of the firm starts to decline. In a world with both taxes and bankruptcy costs, the optimal level of debt would be exactly where any additional gain from using debt is exactly offset by the expected costs associated with bankruptcy.

The probability of financial distress varies from firm to firm and is influenced by factors such as the size of operating cash flows in relation to debt obligations, the proportion of fixed to variable costs or the sensitivity of a firm's cash flows to the general economic activity (Arnold, 2002). In addition, direct bankruptcy costs would generally be lower if a firm has divisible assets or if an external entity such as the government or a cross holding provides support in the case of financial distress. These kinds of cross holdings, in which a group of firms invest in one another and provide support if any of them get into financial trouble, are very common among German companies.

However, financial distress does not automatically mean bankruptcy and not every firm that fails to make its interest payment is forced into liquidation. In some cases lenders agree to delay these payments in return for a higher future interest rate or a controlling share in the company. No matter how, if a firm fails to meet its commitments, stockholders will lose some or all of their control over the firm and it is exactly this fear of loss that becomes the overriding principle when a company decides how to construct its capital structure (Damodaran, 2001). Nevertheless, with taxes and bankruptcy costs an optimal capital structure appears to exist, but Miller (1977) also notes that calculation of such an optimum is extremely complex and is additionally influenced by institutional restrictions and other market imperfections.

3.4 Additional theories and capital market imperfections

3.4.1 Trade-off theory and agency costs

As examined above, optimal capital structure is often thought of as a trade-off between the benefits of debt and the risks and costs of financial distress. Optimal capital structure is determined by trading off the benefits of debt against the risks of financial distress and agency costs. This conflict has been recognised by the trade-off theory of capital structure, which suggests that firms have a target debt to equity ratio and make their financing decision according to their optimum (Drobetz and Fix, 2003). If adjusting capital structure is without cost, each firm would always be at its optimum. However, there are costs, and consequently delays in adjusting capital structure and firms cannot anticipate the random events that drive them away from their capital structure targets. With no flotation costs, adjusting capital structure would be quick and without cost but with floating costs, especially for equity, actual debt ratios usually fluctuate around the target levels. Accordingly, it seems likely that an optimal capital structure exists but is within a target range rather than being an exact amount of debt in capital structure (Brealey and Myers, 1996).

The trade-off theory helps to explain many industry differences in capital structure. It helps to explain why high growth companies with risky assets have low debt in capital structure and mature companies with stable income and safe tangible assets have high leverage ratios. It also helps to explain why some takeovers of well established cash generating companies are financed primarily through debt, as in the case of a leverage-buyout[11]. However, the trade-off theory cannot explain why some of the most profitable and well established companies within an industry have very low debt ratios and give up some of their potential interest tax shields, even though their corporate income tax liabilities are very high (Brealey and Myers, 1996). Within the German P&H industry, Schwarz Pharma AG is such a highly profitable company with excellent credit ratings but very low debt ratios. Here, the trade-off theory fails to explain this present practice of corporate finance.

Another explanation as to why managers decide to take on certain levels of debt is related to the theory of agency costs, in which capital structure is determined by interest conflicts between the providers of debt and equity capi-

---

[11] Leverage-buyouts are acquisitions of public companies which are dominantly financed with debt.

tal (principals) and managers (agents). Agency costs could generally be defined as the direct and indirect costs of ensuring that agents act in the best interest of their principals. It covers costs such as monitoring, reporting and bonding, which are related to the protection of debt holders against expropriation or bankruptcy (Arnold, 2002). In this context, Jensen and Meckling (1976) identify two types of conflicts that can be considered in the theory of capital structure: conflicts between shareholders and mangers and conflicts between debt holders and shareholders.

Firstly, there is the risk that managers are not acting in the interest of shareholders. This conflict arises because managers hold less than 100% of a firm's equity and do not capture the entire gain from their activities. They may therefore be tempted to participate in the firm's profits by transferring some of the firm's resources for their own personal benefit and consume more than the optimal level of consumption (Harris and Raviv, 1991). This inefficiency reduces some of the market value of the firm and diminishes shareholder value. The extent of these conflicts is generally smaller the larger the fraction of a firm's equity is owned by managers. Assuming a constant absolute investment in the firm held by the management, any additional debt in capital structure would increase their equity share and mitigate the effect of these conflicts of interest. Moreover, managers of mature companies with few growth opportunities and large amounts of free cash flow may use these funds to sustain growth or to build *"empires"* at the expense of the firm's profitability. Debt financing could thereby simply add value and mitigate these conflicts by reducing the amount of free cash flows, imposing financial discipline and restricting managers' flexibility to waste excess funds. Furthermore, leverage obliges managers contractually to make interest and principal payments and is therefore more reliable in encouraging managers to be more efficient and to return excess capital to investors. Accordingly, debt reduces the conflicts between managers and equity holders and decreases the agency cost related to the managerial flexibility and inefficient investment projects due to excess amounts of free cash flows (Drobetz and Fix, 2003).

Secondly, debt holders may face an agency problem with shareholders when managers are acting exclusively to maximise shareholder wealth rather than total firm value. The risk shifting hypothesis postulates that there is an incentive for managers acting on behalf of their shareholders to exploit debt holders by investing suboptimally and transferring some wealth from debt holders to shareholders. More specifically, there is an incentive for managers to take on risky projects, which would yield large excess returns for shareholders but no extra return for debt holders. If these investments are successful, equity holders capture most of the gain but if they fail, debt holders bear equal or even most of the costs. This is even more obvious when a firm is already in financial distress. Shareholders have nothing to lose from taking on risky investments but debt holders gain no extra return and additionally lose some value of their claims on the value of the firm in the case of liquidation. Moreover, using option pricing theory, equity could also be seen as a call option on the firm's total value, giving stockholders the right to buy back the firm on maturity of the debt, since they have the option of whether to renegotiate the debt contracts or not. In this context, there is an incentive for managers to accept risky projects or a greater variance of the underlying firm value in order to increase the value of the call option which consequently increases shareholder wealth[12]. In particular, managers tend to accept risky net present value (NPV) projects, which increase the value of equity but decrease some of the value of the debt contracts via the risk and return dimension. The strategy of increasing shareholder wealth by investing excess capital into risky projects is known as the "*overinvestment*" problem (Drobetz and Fix, 2003).

---

[12] Option pricing theory postulates that the value of an option increases as the risk or the standard deviation (σ) of the underlying asset, in this case the firm value, increases and declines when variability decreases [See Van Horne (1998) Ch. 5 and pp. 271 for more detailed information].

On the other hand, there may also be an incentive problem concerning good investment opportunities when a company finances these with debt. Managers acting on the shareholder's behalf may tend to avoid positive NPV projects, which would work more to the benefit of the debt holder than shareholder wealth. This may be the case for projects that lower the overall risk of a firm and enhance debt holder wealth at the expense of shareholder wealth in terms of risk and return considerations or volatility of the underlying firm value. Accordingly, there is a rational reason to reject a positive NPV project, when lenders benefit more and shareholders have no chance to receive any extra gain. Myers (1977) describes this incentive issue as the *"underinvestment"* problem.

The risk shifting hypothesis illustrates the need for debt holders to monitor the actions of managers and explains why lenders impose certain covenants on a firm to protect their position from an increase of risk. But these monitoring activities are costly and require some of the firm's resources. Given that monitoring activities are to some extent imperfect, debt holders anticipate some of these costs by charging higher spreads ex-ante to compensate for possible wealth expropriation ex-post. Shareholders participate in these costs through a lower firm value and managers are confronted with limitations and restrictions on their managerial freedom to act. Thus the increase of leverage increases the implicit cost of debt and lowers the value of a firm. Accordingly, there is a trade-off between the benefits of debt and monitoring costs; a firm needs to find a balance between the savings related to debt and the increase of monitoring and bankruptcy costs (Van Horne, 1998). The financing decision of a firm and its optimal capital structure are now determined by trading off the benefits of debt against agency costs and the previously discussed bankruptcy costs.

The agency theory helps to explain why some successful companies have low leverage ratios and why managers try to limit the amount of debt in capital structure. This is primarily due to the fact that managers do not like external restrictions and limitations. Moreover, highly innovative companies with many growth options are likely to suffer the greatest loss in value if they have to forgo investment opportunities due to a loss of flexibility. The agency theory consequently provides a useful explanation as to why successful companies in highly innovative industries like Schwarz Pharma AG have historically maintained a low debt ratio, even if their cash generating ability supports more debt. In addition, the agency theory suggests that firms with highly divisible assets or investment opportunities should generally have higher debt ratios since monitoring and agency costs as well as the expected cost of financial distress are smaller. In contrast, companies with intransparent investment projects or intangible assets should generally have low leverage ratios.

Agency costs could be generally reduced by stockholder meetings and auditing activities. In Germany, the close link between industry and the banking sector increases the quality of information and lowers the costs of potential agency problems. Furthermore, it is also usual for banks to have directors in supervisory boards and to employ industry specialists who give advice to clientele firms. This mitigates potential agency problems but does not negate the conflict between stockholders and bondholders. Moreover, this may create a conflict through collusion of interests as banks try to maximise the total return on their relationship. Agency problems could generally be reduced through variable pay components such as stock options which align the goal of managers and shareholders and mitigate these conflicts of interest.

3.4.2   Information costs and the pecking order theory

The theory of agency costs is closely related to the problem of information asymmetry, which suggests that managers possess better information about the firm's future income stream than investors. This information disparity between insiders (managers) and outsiders (security holders) is the basis of two related but distinct theories of financing known as "*financial signalling*" and the "*pecking order theory*" (Barkley and Smith, 1999).

The first approach argues that managers may use capital structure changes to signal information about the firm's intrinsic value to security holders. As managers have better information about the firm than investors, the situation could occur where the intrinsic value of the company is greater than the market value of its shares. In this case, managers would try to raise the firm's share price by communicating to the market that the company is currently undervalued. However, it is obviously difficult to find a credible signalling mechanism that provides sufficient evidence for investors to believe that managers are revealing the truth. Economic theory suggests that the financing decision of a firm is one potential signalling device to reveal management information to investors. Ross (1977) suggests that an increase in leverage conveys a positive signal to investors and should lead to a rise in share price. This stems form the fact that debt contracts increase the firm's financial obligations and its probability of bankruptcy. Since managers often suffer most if bankruptcy occurs, investors conclude that they are confident about the firm's future prospects and future cash flows. On the other hand, equity is more forgiving and managers are not obliged to pay dividends and can cut or omit them in times of under performance or financial distress. For this reason, increasing leverage implies a positive signal to investors about the quality of a firm and its future prospects (Drobetz and Fix, 2003). Several economists suggest that announcements of new equity issues lead to a general decline in stock prices. In contrast, the market responds in a systematically positive fashion to announcements of new debt issues. Accordingly, asymmetric information helps to explain why in practice debt financing is, to some extent, preferred over new equity issues.

Myers and Majluf (1984) provide a theoretical explanation as to why the market might interpret new equity issues as "*bad news*". They suggest that managers would generally issue equity instead of debt when they believe that the firm is overvalued and debt instead of equity when they believe the firm is undervalued. This behavioural explanation is further supported by the argument that managers, acting on the shareholders' behalf, would experience an opportunity loss if new shares were issued below their intrinsic value. Conversely, issuing overvalued shares would result in a net gain for existing shareholders, even if the negative signalling effect dilutes some of their stock value. In addition, general empirical evidence suggests that the announcement of leverage-increasing transactions leads to an increase in stock prices and the announcement of leverage-reducing transactions leads to a predictable negative reaction in the market [see e.g. Eckbo and Masulis (1995) or Smith (1986)]. However, it is important to note that whether a firm is over or undervalued, the drop in value after the announcement of an equity issue represents a dilution of existing shareholder interests, which can be referred to as the signalling or information costs of raising external capital (Barkley and Smith, 1999).

Thus, asymmetric information favours debt over equity financing and helps to explain why managers prefer to issue debt. However, asymmetric information is not always important and equity issues are particularly useful for companies with high growth potential. Furthermore, equity issues make sense for firms with heavy borrowings by improving their debt capacity and decreasing their costs and risk of financial distress. Additionally, managers could shore up the firms financial resources for hard times ahead instead of sacrificing valuable investment opportunities in the future. Even if the negative signalling effect dilutes the value of the existing stock, equity is particularly valuable due to its secure nature.

The problem of asymmetric information and the signalling effect of financing lead to the theory of a pecking order in finance, in which firms follow a financing hierarchy and maximise their value by systematically choosing to finance their investments by the easiest and least expense source of financing. Specifically, the pecking order theory of financing suggests that information costs associated with external financing outweigh all other considerations in the firm's financing decision. The pecking order theory, first proposed by Donaldson (1961) and further developed by Myers (1984) and Myers and Majluf (1984), argues against an optimal capital structure and suggests that firms try to finance in the easiest and least costly way with internally generated funds first, then low-risk debt and finally equity. Accordingly, managers avoid issuing undervalued securities by first financing with internal equity funds; predominately retained earnings. Only when their internal funds are insufficient, they would start with bank debt and debt securities, then possible hybrid securities such as convertible bonds and finally ordinary common stock. This theory contrasts sharply with the theories in which an optimal capital structure and a well defined target leverage ratio exist because there are two types of equity, internal and external, one at the top and one at the bottom of the pecking order theory. Each firm's debt ratio consequently reflects its cumulative requirements for external finance and not its well defined target ratio or optimum (Myers, 1984).

The pecking order theory is mainly a behavioural explanation of the capital structure decision. It is consistent with the arguments of asymmetric information and signalling, as well as the issuing costs of finance. Moreover, it helps to explain why the most profitable firms within an industry tend to have the lowest debt ratios. This is due to the fact that they have sufficient internally generated funds to finance their investment opportunities and do not need outside finance. Less profitable companies, on the other hand, generally have more debt in capital structure because they do not have sufficient internally generated funds to finance their growth opportunities. Following the pecking order of financing they use low cost debt as the first alternative due to its low flotation and information costs and only issue equity when their debt capacity is exhausted (Barkley and Smith, 1999). However, when there is an imbalance of internal funds and real investment opportunities, even profitable firms would issue debt or external equity in order to finance potential value enhancing investment projects. In addition, retained earnings also have an opportunity cost for shareholders, and managers must be aware that they need to earn at least the equivalent amount of return that shareholders could earn by investing these funds in the market.

The pecking order theory helps to explain changes in many mature firms' debt ratios but is less successful in explaining industry differences. Mature firms' debt ratios tend to increase when firms have financial deficits and tend to decline when they have sufficient free cash flows. However, it does not explain why debt ratios tend to be low in high-tech and high-growth industries and why there are also companies that do not use their cash surpluses to pay off debt but return these cash flows back to shareholders instead (Brealey and Myers, 1996).

4 Empirical evidence of capital structure theory and corporate practice

4.1 Trade-off theory and the costs and benefits of debt

Among the main competing theories of optimal capital structure are the static trade-off and the pecking order theory. The static trade-off theory assumes that firms have an optimal capital structure and make their financing decision according to their leverage target. Optimal capital structure is thereby determined by weighing the potential benefits of using debt against the risks and costs of financial distress.

Most of the evidence of corporate financing behaviour suggests that firms have a target debt to equity ratio and adjust their capital structures according to this optimum. In addition, numerous studies indicate that leverage ratios are industry related, given that leverage ratios of firms within an industry tend to be more similar than leverage ratios across industries. For example, Schwartz and Aronson (1967) as well as Long and Malitz (1985) analyse leverage ratios across industries and provide evidence supporting the conclusion that leverage ratios are related to specific industry characteristics. The study by Long and Malitz (1985) shows that mature and asset intensive industries, such as steel or cement, are highly leveraged, whereas high growth industries, such as drugs or cosmetics, have consistently low leverage ratios. This result is further supported by a study from Harris and Raviv (1991), which summarises several studies on industry leverage ratios using data from the United States (US). Their ranking of industries by leverage shows that drugs, cosmetics and instruments have consistently the lowest leverage ratios, whereas electric and gas utilities, telephone and steel have generally the highest leverage ratios. Furthermore, their study suggests that leverage generally increases with fixed assets, growth opportunities, non-debt tax shields and firm size and that it is negatively correlated with volatility, profitability, the probability of bankruptcy, R&D and advertising expenditure and the uniqueness of the product.[13] In addition, a related study by Rajan and Zingales (1995) using international data, suggests that at an aggregate level, firm leverage is fairly similar across the G-7 countries, despite institutional differences that influence firm and industry leverage across countries. Moreover, they find that the factors correlated with leverage in the US appear to be similarly relevant for firms across the G-7 countries as well.

Theoretical models of capital structure further suggest that in practice interest and non-debt tax shields influence corporate debt policies. DeAngelo and Masulis (1980) demonstrate in their model of capital structure that non-debt related tax shields such as depreciation, amortisation or investment tax credits are perfect substitutes for interest tax shields related to debt financing. Accordingly, firms with more taxable income and fewer non-debt tax shields should have higher leverage ratios, whereas firms with lower income and higher non-debt tax shields should have lower leverage ratios. Furthermore, their model suggests that an optimal capital structure exists on a firm and industry level since tax rates and non-debt tax shields vary across industries and depend on industry and firm specific characteristics. However, the evidence of tax shields and leverage provides no clear, or at least only moderate, support of their importance in explaining capital structures and debt policies in practice.

For instance Bowen et al. (1982) and Kim and Sorensen (1986) support DeAngelo's and Masulis' (1980) hypothesis that more non-debt tax shields lead to a lower amount of debt in capital structure and show that non-debt tax shields are negatively related to leverage. In addition, a recent cross sectional study by Chen and Jiang (2001), testing determinants of capital structure choice for Dutch firms by structural equation modelling, suggests that non-debt tax shields (measured by the provision ratio) are important ex-

---

[13] More detailed explanation of these factors and their application to theory can be found in section 4.4 Determinants and attributes of capital structure choice.

planatory factors of leverage. They show that non-debt tax shields are negatively correlated with leverage and support the practical relevance of DeAngelo's and Masulis' hypothesis for Dutch firms. In contrast, Bradley et al. (1984) and Chaplinsky and Niehaus (1990) do not support these results and show instead a positive relation between leverage and non-debt tax shields for firms in the US, which disproves the practical relevance of DeAngelos and Masuls' hypothesis.

Additional empirical work by Cordes and Sheffrin (1983) suggests that various tax codes and different tax rates across industries explain some of the inter-industry similarities. They examine cross sectional differences in effective tax rates caused by factors such as tax carry-backs and carry-forwards, foreign tax credits and investment tax credits, and find that significant differences exist across industries in the US. In addition, Mackie-Mason (1990) shows that firms with high marginal tax rates are more likely to issue debt, whereas firms with low marginal tax rates are more likely to issue equity. Furthermore, Graham (1996) provides evidence that debt ratios and marginal tax rates are positively correlated. His study analyses the relationship between changes in leverage and tax rates in a sample of 10,000 firms in the US between 1980 and 1992 and finds that firms with higher tax rates are more likely to issue debt. This further highlights the importance of interest tax shields as an explanatory factor of corporate financing behaviour.

Capital structure theory further suggests that the direct and indirect costs of bankruptcy are important determinants of capital structure. Warner (1977) examines the direct costs of bankruptcy on a number of US railroad companies and finds that the direct costs associated with the administration of the bankruptcy process are trivial, averaging about 1% of the firm's market values seven years prior and 5.3% immediately prior to bankruptcy. Accordingly, Warner concludes that the expected direct costs of bankruptcy are far too low to be significant in explaining corporate debt policies in practice.

Furthermore, he indicates that bankruptcy costs decrease with size and smaller companies have considerably higher proportional bankruptcy costs than their larger counterparts. This indicates economics of scale in the administration of the bankruptcy process and suggests that leverage ratios may be related to firm size. However, his conclusion on the irrelevancy of bankruptcy costs is inconclusive because it does not consider the indirect costs of bankruptcy which are often much greater than the more obvious direct bankruptcy costs. In contrast, Weiss (1990) investigated 31 bankruptcies in the US between 1980 and 1986 and revealed average bankruptcy costs of 20% of the firm's equity market value in the year prior to bankruptcy. In addition, Altman (1984) investigated the relevance of indirect bankruptcy costs (measured by an estimate of profits) using a time-series regression and suggests indirect bankruptcy costs of about 8.1% of the firm value three years prior to bankruptcy which increase to 10.5% one year prior to bankruptcy. These results suggest that bankruptcy costs are significant and have to be considered as a cost of leverage in corporate finance.

Additional cross sectional work by Bradley et al. (1984) and Titman and Wessels (1988) provide further evidence that bankruptcy costs are, to some extent, important determinants of financial leverage. Their empirical work shows that leverage is significantly negatively correlated with the probability of bankruptcy (measured by the volatility of earnings) and corporate growth opportunities (measured by R&D and advertising expenditures). Accordingly, they suggest that bankruptcy and growth are important for explaining capital structure choice in practice. Another study by Drobetz and Fix (2003) indicates a similar negative correlation between leverage and the probability of bankruptcy (measured by the volatility of earnings) for firms in Switzerland. Furthermore, they show by using a simple target adjustment regression model that Swiss firms have long term financial targets and conclude that their results are consistent with the static trade-off theory.

Collectively, the empirical evidence on tax and bankruptcy costs provides moderate support for the practical relevance of the trade-off theory. The evidence of target capital structures and industry groupings in leverage ratios suggests that optimal capital structure depends on industry specific characteristics. Numerous studies explain these similarities with the tax shield hypothesis and imply that various tax codes and different tax rates are the reason for these inter-industry similarities. In spite of evidence of tax shields, there may also be other industry similarities, such as growth rates, earnings volatility or the asset structure that may explain the relationship between industry membership and capital structure in practice. Moreover, the evidence regarding bankruptcy costs suggests that they are significant in explaining optimal capital structure as a trade-off between the gains from leverage and the expected costs of financial distress.

4.2   Evidence of asymmetric information, signalling and the pecking order

The theory of asymmetric information argues that informational disparity between managers and investors is the reason why new equity issues are less desirable than new debt issues. The signalling theory extends this argument and postulates that capital structure signals management information about the firm's future prospects to investors. Managers decide to issue equity when they assume that the firm is overvalued and debt when they assume that the firm is undervalued. The pecking order theory extends these arguments and suggests that mangers tend to avoid external finance whenever possible. It implies that there is no optimal or target capital structure and firms follow a financing hierarchy by choosing to finance their investment opportunities in the easiest and least costly way with internally generated funds first, then low-risk debt and finally equity.

The plausibility of the signalling theory has been empirically investigated by several time series studies, testing the announcement effects of diverse corporate events on equity prices. Most empirical evidence for signalling [see e.g. Smith (1986) or Dietrich (1984)] suggests that leverage increasing events have a significantly positive effect on equity prices whereas leverage decreasing events have a significantly negative effect on stock prices. Furthermore, announcements that imply favourable future cash flow changes such as an increase in investment or dividend payouts generally have a positive effect on shareholder wealth, whereas contrary announcements evoke the opposite effect (Copeland et al, 2004). In addition, Baker and Wurgler (2002) demonstrate that firms tend to issue equity when their market values (measured by their relative market-to-book values and past market values) are high and repurchase equity when their market values are relatively low which supports the asymmetric information hypothesis and indicates that managers and investors have different perceptions of the intrinsic value of the firm.

Moreover, numerous studies support the pecking order theory by demonstrating that past profitability and leverage are negatively correlated. For example, Titman and Wessels (1988) and Rajan and Zingales (1995) provide empirical evidence that there is a negative relationship between profitability and debt ratios. In contrast, Long and Malitz (1985) do not find this relationship. Furthermore, Kim and Sorensen (1986) show that leverage is negatively correlated to corporate growth which indicates that slow growth firms generally have lower levels of debt than their high growth counterparts. Moreover, Shyam-Sunder and Myers (1999) test the static trade-off against the pecking order theory by linear regression analysis and conclude that the time-series variance of debt explains more of a firm's debt ratio than a simple target leverage adjustment model. Accordingly, they conclude that managers do not set target leverage ratios, which is consistent with the pecking order theory. However, Chirinko and Singha (2000) criticise their conclusion and point out that it is difficult to test these theories with the experimental design of their regression analysis. Another study by Frank and Goyal (2003) tests the pecking order theory by examining the relative importance of 39 different factors on the firm's leverage decision. They suggest that financing deficits have no predictive power on the decision to raise external capital, which is to some extent consistent with the pecking order theory. Another study by Minton and Wruck (2001) analyses a group of firms in the US that follow financial conservatism and finds that those firms with very low leverage ratios tend to have larger amounts of internal funds. Furthermore, they find that when these firms raise external funds they tend to choose to issue debt, which is consistent with the pecking order hypothesis. In contrast, these firms tend not to exhaust all of their internal funds before they start to issue external funds. Contrary to the predictions of the trade-off theory, they observe that the debt policies of these firms cannot be explained by the tax shields hypothesis, given that the investigated firms do not have consistently low tax rates or high non-debt tax shields.

Besides their evidence for the static trade-off theory, Drobetz and Fix (2003) also find that more profitable firms use less leverage, which is consistent with the pecking order theory. They suggest that the strong positive correlation between leverage and investment opportunities (measured by the book-to-market equity ratio) is consistent with both the pecking order and the trade-off theory. Chen and Jiang (2001) demonstrate a similar result for both theories and show that financial flexibility (measured by the ratio of cash and marketable securities over current assets) is negatively correlated to financial leverage. Based on the fact that they define financial flexibility as internal debt, they conclude that the pecking order theory partially explains the corporate financing behaviour of Dutch firms. However, asymmetric information does not seem to be the driving force behind the evidence of the pecking order theory, since growth and leverage are consistently positively correlated; exactly the opposite of what the theory of asymmetric information suggests.

The empirical evidence on asymmetric information, signalling and the pecking order theory provides mixed results in their relevance in explaining debt policies in practice. The evidence of signalling suggests that markets tend to assess capital structure changes and leverage related announcements in the way signalling theory predicts; accordingly it seems that the market assumes asymmetric information. Furthermore, the evidence concerning the pecking order theory provides at least moderate support that it is useful in explaining the financing behaviour of some companies, particularly mature and conservative firms. Nevertheless, several studies argue against the pecking order hypothesis and provide opposing evidence.

Collectively, the empirical results provide moderate evidence for both the pecking order and the trade-off theory and suggest that they are not mutually exclusive and are both useful in explaining the debt policies of some firms and industries in practice. However, up to now, financial theorists have not found a universal empirical test that explains corporate financing behaviour in total and is powerful enough to distinguish itself among the competing theories. Furthermore, it should also be pointed out that capital structure is difficult to test empirically, perhaps due to the fact that the theoretical attributes are abstract and not directly observable. Changes in capital structure often come along with new investment opportunities and it is nearly impossible to effectively assess their impact on firm value by statistical modelling techniques. Moreover, it is hard to get good market value data and difficult to identify homogeneous measures of capital structure proxies due to differences in accounting practices. Therefore, it could be argued that these quantitative modelling approaches provide insufficient evidence on the practical relevance of capital structure theories. Accordingly, the following section introduces two cross sectional studies on capital structure theory, based on empirical surveys.

4.3   What practitioners think about capital structure theory

Although there is a large body of cross sectional evidence on optimal capital structure by regression or structural linear modelling, more recent research focuses on cross sectional analysis by empirical surveys to identify how capital structure theory can be used to determine the finance behaviour of companies.

Graham and Harvey (2001) surveyed 392 chief financial officers (CFOs) of US companies about capital structure and its determinants and found moderate support for both the trade-off and the pecking order theory. Their survey shows that 19% of the firms have no debt to equity ratio target, 37% have a flexible target and 44% have a tight or very strict leverage target or capital structure range; about 73.5% of the respondents report that they always or almost always use the CAPM to estimate their cost of equity capital. Most of the CFOs consider the tax advantage of debt as moderately important in their financial policy, but are not directly concerned about personal taxes or the potential cost of financial distress. This provides at least moderate support for the practical relevance of the trade-off theory. Furthermore, their survey provides little evidence about the theory that agency conflicts, such as underinvestment costs or corporate control considerations affect capital structure choice in practice. It also illustrates that financial flexibility and equity undervaluation are important determinants of capital structure and security issuance, which is in general consistent with the pecking order theory; but the arguments related to asymmetric information are not the driving forces for their importance. Moreover, their study shows little evidence that managers consider the information effects of signalling as important. However, their analysis illustrates that informal criteria such as credit ratings, earnings volatility and financial flexibility are the most important factors when managers decide on their firm's debt policy.

Another very similar survey by Bancel and Mittoo (2002) investigates capital structure decision and its determinants in 17 European countries. They find that about three quarters of the firms have a target leverage ratio and calculate their cost of capital and 70 percent of them use the CAPM to calculate their cost of equity. Most of the managers attach importance to the weighted average cost of capital and the tax advantage of debt, but these are not the driving forces behind their debt policy. The transaction costs of debt and the timing of debt and equity issues are also deemed as moderately important, but few managers would postpone the issue of new debt and equity because of these factors. On the other hand, potential costs of distress, industry norms of debt and agency costs have no importance in their financing decision. Accordingly, these factors provide mixed support for the argument that companies trade-off the benefits of debt against the costs of distress and agency to derive their optimal capital structure. Furthermore, they find little support for the signalling and the pecking order theory, given that managers do not consider the signalling effects of debt and equity issues as important. The most important factors that influence corporate debt policies are financial flexibility, credit rating and the tax advantage of debt. Additionally, when issuing equity, managers are concerned about earnings per share dilution, the level of interest rates and the market value of their stock when issuing equity and selecting the timing of debt and equity issues.

The analysis of these two empirical surveys provides moderate support for the trade-off theory but little evidence for the pecking order theory. In addition, these studies reveal that informal criteria, such as financial flexibility, credit rating or earnings per share dilution are the most important factors that affect corporate debt policy, new security issues and capital structure in practice.

4.4   Determinants of capital structure

Taking a closer look at the results of the study by Rajan and Zingales (1995), it is quite obvious that differences in institutional settings have some relevance in explaining differences in capital structure choice across the G-7 countries. Important institutional factors that may influence capital structure at an aggregate level are tax laws, bankruptcy code, financial institutions and corporate governance issues.

Not surprisingly, German tax rules have a strong impact on accounting practice, influencing financial decisions such as the valuation of assets and liabilities, the measurement of profits and depreciation and the calculation of bad debt and other provisions (Nobes, 1996). For example, the position of provisions is a German peculiarity, which influences a significant proportion of the right-hand side of the balance sheet. This term covers different types of accounting reserves, whether for tax, development costs, bad debts or pensions. Most of them are part of long term liabilities (for example pensions) while others are part of stockholder equity (for example tax concessions). Future pension liabilities are therefore a significant proportion of provisions for German firms (about 14% of the firm's total liabilities in 1981), which are often retained and invested in physical assets and inflate the book value of both total assets and total liabilities (Rutterford, 1988). Besides German tax regulations that dominate accounting rules and lead to a conservative accounting practice in Germany, capital structure is furthermore influenced by the pertinent corporate and personal income tax regulations. As explained above, high German personal tax rates (up to 56%) suggest that tax-exempt investors would experience debt as more favourable, whereas personal investors should generally favour equity, particularly capital gains.

Another peculiarity of the German system is the important role of financial institutions in corporate debt financing. According to De Bondt (1998), banks and financial institutions account for 94% of total loans to the private sector; banks alone account for 89% of total loans to the private sector. In addition, universal banks are both debt and equity investors (about 9% of total equity finance in 1988) and are closely linked to the corporate sector via cross holdings, the exchange of personnel and directors on the supervisory board (Rutterford 1988).

Several economists [see e.g. White (1993) and Kaiser (1994)] argue that the creditor friendly German bankruptcy code is not conducive to restructure firms. In the event of bankruptcy, firms are very likely to be liquidated rather than reorganised. Since liquidation values are generally lower than going concern values, potential bankruptcy costs are considered to be more costly in Germany. Nonetheless, the close relationship between creditors and debtors and the close links of the corporate sector via inter-company cross holdings reduce information asymmetries and the probability of financial distress.

Another institutional characteristic of the German market is the level of concentration of ownership and the market for corporate control. Ownership is highly concentrated in the German market due to inter-company cross holdings or dual class stock. In addition, takeover defences are broadly used by German companies. According to Franks and Mayer (1994), attempts at hostile takeovers in the German market are rare; they report three attempts in the period after the Second World War.

Several studies on optimal capital structure [see e.g. Harris and Raviv (1991) and Rajan and Zingales (1995)] suggest that leverage is cross sectionally correlated with certain attributes. The following analysis focuses on six of these variables, including tangibility of assets (the ratio of fixed to total assets), growth opportunities (the market-to-book ratio), firm size (natural logarithm of sales), profitability (return on average equity), volatility (variability of sales 5Yr moving average) and non-debt tax shields (ratio of depreciation, depletion and amortisation expenses to total assets).

(i) Tangibility

Most capital structure theories suggest that the composition of assets owned by a firm influences their choice of capital structure. The theory of agency costs suggests that managers of highly levered firms, acting on behalf of shareholders, tend to invest suboptimally and expropriate wealth from debt holders which causes the classical shareholder-bondholder conflict [see e.g. Galai and Masulis (1976); Jensen and Meckling (1976) and Myers (1977)].

48

However, if a large fraction of a firm's assets is tangible, the firm can use its assets to collateralize its debt, which restricts the management in using free funds and consequently diminishes the agency conflicts between shareholders and lenders (Titman and Wessels 1988). Hence creditors have a higher guarantee of repayment and retain more value in the case of liquidation. In addition, creditors are more willing to supply loans and the firm's debt capacity and the expected level of debt should therefore increase. Accordingly, the agency theory suggests a positive correlation between the tangibility of assets and the level of debt in capital structure.

Another agency conflict arises from the tendency of managers to consume more than the optimal level of consumption. Grossman and Hart (1982) argue that higher levels of debt mitigate this problem, because monitoring activities of bondholders and bankers restrict managers' flexibility. Furthermore, higher levels of debt impose financial discipline due to a reduction in the amount of free cash flows and increase the probability of financial distress. The cost of this agency conflict is probably higher for firms with lower levels of collateralizable assets, since monitoring the capital outlay is more difficult and consequently more expensive. Therefore, firms with lower levels of collateralizable assets may choose higher levels of debt and one can expect a negative relationship between tangibility of assets and leverage (Titman and Wessels 1988).

Previous empirical studies by Titman and Wessels (1988), Rajan and Zingales (1995) and Drobetz and Fix (2003) argue that the ratio of fixed to total assets is a useful proxy for tangibility. This analysis uses the ratio of total property, plant and equipment to total assets as a proxy for tangibility. Total property, plant and equipment includes all tangible assets with an expected useful life of over one year and total assets represents the sum of total current assets, net value of property plant and equipment and other long term assets and long term receivables investments.

The Theory of Capital Structure

(ii) Size

Numerous authors suggest that firm size is positively related to leverage. Warner (1977) provides evidence that the direct costs of bankruptcy are inversely related to firm size and suggests that bankruptcy costs decrease as firm size increases. In addition, Titman and Wessels (1988) argue that larger firms are more diversified and less likely to be susceptible to financial distress. Accordingly, larger firms should be more leveraged than smaller firms and size should be positively correlated with leverage. Given that size can be regarded as an indirect proxy for the probability of bankruptcy, this positive correlation is consistent with the trade-off theory, since lower bankruptcy costs increase the tax advantage of debt. Moreover, this relationship is also consistent with the arguments of information asymmetry, which suggest that bigger firms have fewer informational disparities and therefore better access to debt capital markets (Chen and Jiang, 2001). On the other hand, larger firms also have better access to equity markets and lower transaction costs associated with issuing equity, which may increase their preference for equity. The arguments of information asymmetry also suggest a negative correlation between leverage and firm size and larger firms may be less leveraged than smaller firms (Drobetz and Fix, 2003).

As proposed in Titman and Wessels (1988), Rajan and Zingales (1995) and Drobetz and Fix (2003) this analysis uses the natural logarithm of sales as a proxy for size. Sales is thereby defined as gross sales and other operating revenues (net) minus discounts, returns and allowances. The logarithm transformation accounts thereby for a size effect in sales, which particularly affects small firms.

(iii) Growth opportunities

As mentioned previously, highly levered firms have a tendency to invest suboptimally and to transfer some wealth from debt holders to shareholders. Firms in growing industries are likely to have higher agency costs, since they need more flexibility in their choice of future investments (Titman and

Wessels 1988). Furthermore, high growth firms are likely to suffer the greatest loss if they have to pass up profitable investment opportunities. Therefore, firms with high growth opportunities might find debt too costly and use a greater amount of equity finance. Given that debt limits financial flexibility, leverage should be negatively correlated to future growth opportunities. This result is also consistent with the trade-off theory which predicts that high growth firms have a stronger incentive to avoid under investment problems which arise from stockholder/bondholder conflicts (Drobetz and Fix, 2003). Furthermore, the pecking order theory suggests a negative relationship between leverage and growth, since growing firms with a higher degree of financial flexibility have higher levels of information asymmetry and external funding is more expensive and consequently less desirable.

As proposed in Myers (1977), this investigation uses the ratio of market value of assets (total market capitalisation) to book value of assets as a proxy for investment opportunities. The market value of assets is thereby calculated by multiplying the current number of shares by the company's share price as of the 4th of September 2004. Based on the assumption that stock prices reflect intangible assets such as growth opportunities, high growth companies should have larger average market-to-book values than their low growth counterparts.

(iv) Profitability
Myers (1984) and Myers and Majluf (1984) suggest that firms prefer to follow a pecking order and finance their activities with internally generated funds first, then low-risk debt and finally equity. The behavioural explanation of the pecking order theory is related to the costs associated with external financing, primarily the costs associated with asymmetric information and transaction costs. In this sense, highly profitable firms with slow growth rates should have low leverage ratios and yet not profitable firms with high growth rates should end up with relatively high leverage ratios. Accord-

ingly, the pecking order theory predicts a negative correlation between leverage and past profitability. In contrast, the trade-off theory, agency cost and signalling hypothesis suggest a positive relationship between leverage and profitability. This is based on the fact that more profitable firms have lower expected bankruptcy costs and debt is consequently more favourable than equity. Furthermore, the agency model predicts that higher levels of debt reduce the potential conflicts of interest among principals and managers and impose discipline on the firm's investment policy and its financial flexibility. Signalling theory predicts that managers use higher levels of debt to signal positive information about the quality of the firm and its future prospects, which suggests a positive relationship between leverage and profitability (Drobetz and Fix, 2003). This analysis uses the return on average equity as a proxy for profitability, which is defined as the net income before extraordinary items and preferred dividends to total common equity.

(v) Volatility

Many authors suggest that volatility of earnings is an important determinant of capital structure. The trade-off theory and the pecking order model predict a negative relationship between leverage and earnings volatility since more volatile cash flows increase the probability of bankruptcy and drive up the cost of debt and external funding. This analysis uses the variability of sales as a proxy for volatility, which is defined as the variability of sales in terms of a 5 year moving average.

(vi) Non-debt tax shields

Another model of capital structure by DeAngelo and Masulis (1980) demonstrates that non-debt tax shields, such as depreciation and investment tax credits, are perfect substitutes for the interest tax shields related to debt financing. Accordingly, firms with large non-debt tax shields should have less debt in capital structure and leverage and non-debt tax shields should be negatively correlated. Previous empirical studies by Titman and Wessels (1988) and Drobetz and Fix (2003) use the ratio of total depreciation over total assets as an empirical proxy for non-debt tax shields. For that reason, this study uses the ratio of depreciation, depletion and amortisation expenses over total assets as a measure for non-debt tax shields. However, the identification of a reliable proxy is somewhat problematic and the proposed proxy for non-debt tax shields may also be a measure for other theoretical attributes. For example, firms with more tangible assets have higher depreciation ratios and are more likely to have fewer investment opportunities. Accordingly, the ratio of depreciation could also be perceived as a proxy for growth opportunities and leverage and depreciation should be positively correlated (Ozkan, 2001).

The outlined testable correlations between leverage and its explanatory variables are summarized as following.

TABLE 1:

Theoretical correlations between leverage and its
explanatory variables

Attributes	Trade-off theory (Agency cost, Tax, Bankruptcy cost)	Pecking order theory (Asymmetric information)
Tangibility	(+)/(-)	
Size	(+)	(-)/(+)
Growth opportunities	(-)	(-)
Profitability	(+)	(-)
Non-debt tax shields	(-)	

5 An empirical investigation of determinants of capital structure

5.1 Measurement of capital structure

Two measures of leverage are used in this analysis, the ratio of *"Net Debt to Common Equity"* and the ratio of *"Total Debt to Total Assets"*. The first definition of leverage can be viewed as an indicator of the firm's ability to sell assets in order to repay its debts and may be used as a proxy for the firm's credit risk or risk of default (Arnold, 2002). Net debt is thereby defined as all long term and short term debt, including all interest bearing debt and capitalized leasing expenses, minus cash and short terms investments in the current asset section of the balance sheet. Common equity represents the common shareholders interest in the company, which is similar to the net worth or net asset figure in the balance sheet. The second measure of capital structure (Total Debt to Total Assets) gives some indication of the relative share of the company's total assets belonging to debt holders and shareholders (Arnold, 2002). Total debt covers all long term and short term interest bearing debt and capitalized lease obligations and total assets represents the sum of total current assets and long term assets, long term receivables and investments.

Due to data limitations, all variables are measured in book values and not in market values, except the proxy for growth opportunities which is defined as the ratio of market capitalisation to total assets. The use of book values may perhaps introduce some bias but existing studies demonstrate a high cross sectional correlation between book and market values, which indicates that the inaccuracy of using book values is fairly small. Moreover, corporate treasurers tend to use book values in their financial planning in order to avoid distortions caused by the volatility of market values which may not reflect the intended financial policy adequately. However, the above-introduced measures of debt only cover debt in a narrow sense (interest bearing debt) and fail to incorporate the fact that there are some assets that are offset by specific non-debt liabilities. For example an increase in the gross amount of trade credits results in a reduction of this measure of leverage (Rajan and Zingales, 1995). Furthermore, this measure is influenced by factors that may have nothing to do with financing, such as provision and reserves, which could decrease the measures of leverage when assets are held against pension liabilities.

The following analysis is based on two regression analyses. Given that the statistical results for both measures of leverage are fairly similar, the following part uses the net debt to common equity ratio to illustrate the statistical investigation of determinants of capital structure for the German P&H industry. The basic regression output as well as the tables of correlation for the second definition of leverage (Total Debt to Total Assets) can be found in Appendix 19.

5.2 Characteristics of the sample data

The following section investigates determinants of capital structure by multiple regression analysis. The data on the introduced proxies for the theoretical attributes of capital structure is obtained from Thomson Analytics using Datastream, Thomson Financial and Worldscope databases. The initial sample data is based on 40 listed pharmaceutical and healthcare companies out of the Prime Pharma and Healthcare Index[14]. The P&H industry is selected for this analysis because firms within this industry have very low leverage ratios and the investigation of determinants of capital structure is therefore particularly challenging. Furthermore, the underlying index contains a reasonably mixed sample of large and small firms and the amount of available data is sufficient for the statistical analysis in comparison to other industry indices.

---

[14] This index is for example publicly available on www.onvista.de (Aktien/SucheFinde/Index).

After a first examination of the data set, all non-German firms are excluded from the sample data. Secondly, all firms that do not follow IFRS and US-GAAP are deleted from the data set because these two rules of accounting are generally more comparable than the German accounting rules (HGB). However, even if the ongoing accounting harmonisation strives to bring IFRS and US-GAAP into line, a potential source of bias still arises from possible differences in asset evaluation and profit measurement. In total, the sample of the initial regression model contains 28 firms and 280 observations (Appendix 2).

Preliminary graphical and statistical investigation of the initial regression model reveals observations 2 and 16 as unusual (Appendix 4). After removing observation 2 (AAP Implantate AG) and observation 16 (UMS United Medical Systems International) from the data set the regression model shows significant improvements and R2, R2(adj) and the F value increase from 57.5%, 45.5% and 4.78% to 69.0%, 59.2% and 7.05% (Appendix 5). With regard to these improvements and the statistical tests of the regression model, the following investigation is based upon 26 rather than initial 28 firms.

At first glance, the table of descriptive statistic shows that the leverage ratios of the investigated P&H companies are generally very low, with an average mean of 0.0231, a maximum of 1.89 and a minimum of -1.090 (Appendix 6). This relates primarily to the large amounts of cash and short term investments which indicate that most of these companies attach importance to financial flexibility and possibly pursue an investment or expansion strategy. Furthermore, it is remarkable that SIZE has a relatively large standard deviation of 1.076 with a maximum of 3.86, a mean of 2.005 and a minimum of 0.00. This indicates that the data set contains a fairly mixed sample of large and small firms and the bias towards one or the other is relatively small.

By analysing the relationship between LEV and its explanatory variables, it is remarkable that there is a strong negative correlation between LEV and GROPP (Appendix 7). The correlation coefficient of r = -0.708 suggests that lower levels of debt could be expected for firms with higher growth opportunities. This is further supported by the hypothesis test of the correlation coefficient's p-value by testing the alternatives H0 - the correlation coefficient is not reliable against H1 - the correlation coefficient is reliable. The null hypothesis H0 can thereby be rejected if the p-value is < 0.05. Given that the p-value of the correlation coefficient is 0.000, H0 can be rejected and it can be concluded that the correlation coefficient is reliable. Furthermore, a weaker positive correlation exists between LEV and SIZE. The correlation coefficient of r = 0.586 suggests that larger firms have higher levels of debt. This is further supported by the hypothesis test of significance of the correlation coefficient's p-value, which suggest that H0 can be rejected given that 0.002 < 0.05.

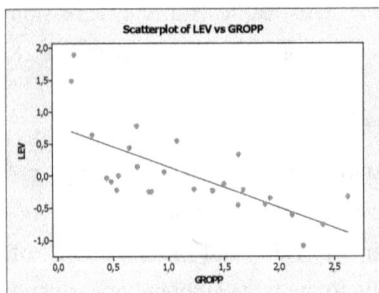

FIGURE 3 Scatter plot of LEV vs. GROPP

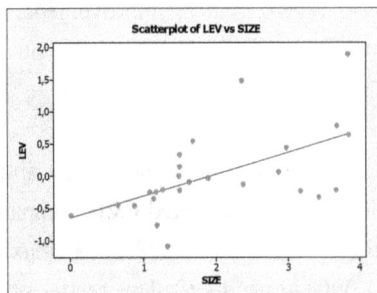

FIGURE 4 Scatter plot of LEV vs. SIZE

Moreover, the analysis of the relationship between the explanatory variables suggests that there is a significant positive correlation between SIZE/PROF and SIZE/TANG with a correlation coefficient of r = 0.633 and r = 0.412. This suggests that larger firms are generally more profitable and tend to have larger amounts of tangible assets. Furthermore, there is a significant negative correlation between SIZE/VOL, PROF/VOL, GROPP/TANG and PROF/NDTS. The correlation coefficients related to these variables are $r = -0.404$, $r = -0.479$, $r = -0.469$ and $r = -0.411$. This suggests that larger and more profitable firms have less volatile sales, firms with higher growth opportunities have fewer tangible assets and more profitable firms have fewer non-debt tax shields. The significance of these correlation coefficients is further supported by the hypothesis test of the correlation coefficient's p-values, which shows that they are all < 0.05 and H0 can be rejected respectively.

5.3   Linear regression model application and empirical results

5.3.1   Linear regression model selection and interpretation

A linear regression model is a statistical technique that is used to describe relationships among variables (Dielman, 1996). The relationships between the dependent and the independent variables are expressed in form of a basic equation;

$$(10)\ E\ (Y) = \beta 0 + \beta 1\ X1 + \beta 2\ X2 + \ldots + \beta k\ Xk + \varepsilon$$

The X's in the equation (10) replace the variables and the β's (betas) represent the unknown parameters of the regression line, which are estimated by using the specific values out of the data set.

Based on the underlying data set, the linear regression line of best fit is;

$$(11)\ LEV = \beta 0 + \beta 1\ TANG + \beta 2\ SIZE + \beta 3\ GROPP + \beta 4\ PROF + \beta 5\ VOL + \beta 6\ NDTS + \varepsilon$$

The final linear regression equation of best fit of determinants of capital structure for the German P&H industry, in correspondence with the sample data and this analysis is;

$$(12)\ LEV = 0.489 - 0.032\ TANG + 0.248\ SIZE - 0.58\ GROPP - 0.004\ PROF - 0.039\ VOL - 4.74\ NDTS$$

Using the regression equation of best fit (12), the capital structure choice of firms within the German P&H industry could be estimated by the given explanatory variables. The coefficient of determination $R2 = 69.0\%$, suggests that approximately 2/3 of the firm's leverage decision is explained by the regression model. Assuming that an industry optimum exists and that com-

panies move towards this optimum, optimal capital structure could be estimated for any of the P&H companies by using this final regression model
(12). The estimated leverage for Schwarz Pharma AG could now be calculated at 0.07. Thereby it is obvious that the estimated leverage is different
from the actual value of -0.24 but it should be kept in mind that the regression model only estimates LEV in relation to the specific sample data. Other
factors not yet identified or included might additionally influence the true
intercept and slope of the regression model. These possible error factors are
expressed by the stochastic disturbance term ε within the initial regression
model of best fit (11). In addition, the relationship between the data might
not be as linear as the regression analysis assumes and the application of the
mathematical model might therefore not be as accurate as desired. For that
reason, the variability of the model and its assumptions need to be examined
further before the regression equation can be used to estimate capital structure for the German P&H industry.

5.3.2   Interpretation of the regression model results

Having analysed basic statistics and stated the recommended regression
model, this paper now investigates the variability of the mathematical
model statistically. The table of coefficients within the regression analysis
provides some reasonable justification for the suitability of the regression
model (Appendix 5). The coefficient of determination $R^2 = 69.0\%$, which
measures the fit of the regression line, suggests that 69.0% of the total
variation in LEV is explained by the regression model and approximately
1/3 $(1-R^2)$ remains unexplained; R2 adjusted for degrees of freedom is at
59.2%. The relatively low residual standard deviation of $s = 0.41$, which estimates the remaining unexplained variation, gives further evidence of the
good fit of the model. Moreover, the low p-value of the regression model in
the analysis of variance provides further evidence to conclude that the test
statistics of the regression model are reliable. However, the low F value of
7.05, which can be thought of as a test of the significance of the regression

equation and R2, casts doubt on the variability of the regression model application. Nevertheless, the F test at a 5% level of significance shows that H0 can be rejected, given that $7.05 > 2.63^{15}$, which indicates that at least one of the explanatory variables is significant in explaining the variation in LEV (Dielman, 1996).

5.3.3 Preliminary testing of the regression model assumptions

The scatter plot of standardized residuals versus the fitted values reveals no major pattern, which indicates no inadequacy of the regression model (Figure 5).

FIGURE 5:

Scatter plot standardised residuals vs. fitted values

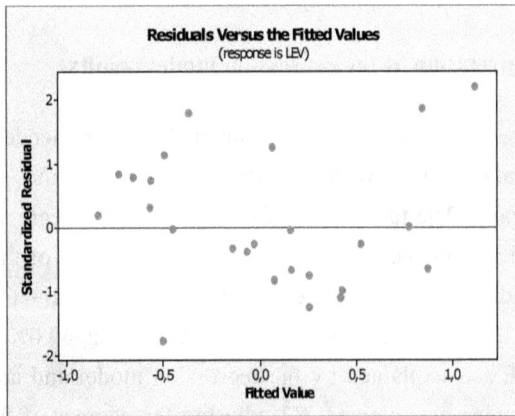

---

[15] F distribution with 19 DF: P(X <= x) = 0.9500; x = 2.62832 (F; 05; 6; 19); based on the decision rule: Reject H0 if F > F (a, K, n-K-1).

Furthermore, the normal probability plot of the residuals shown in Figure 6 indicates that most of the standardized residuals follow an approximately normal distribution.

FIGURE 6:

Normal probability plot of the standardised residuals

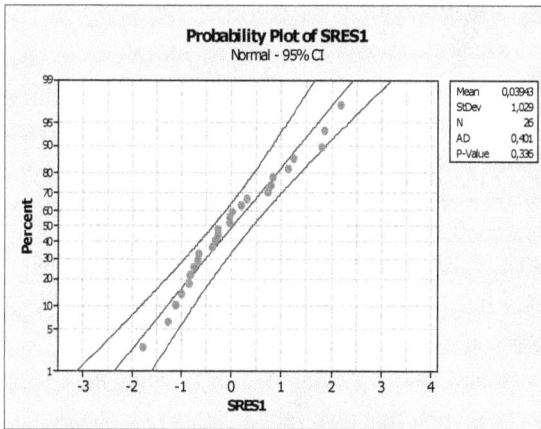

This is additionally supported by the Anderson-Darling, Kolmogorov-Smirnov and the Ryan-Joiner test for normality. The decision rule of hypothesis testing of the normal distribution of the residuals can be stated as: H0 – there is no significant deviation from normality or H1 – there is significant deviation from normality. H0 can be rejected if the p-value is < 0.05. Given that the all p-values are > 0.05 H0 cannot be rejected and it can be concluded that there is sufficient evidence that the residuals follow a normal distribution (Appendix 10).

Furthermore, the plot of residuals versus the explanatory variables does not indicate a violation of the assumed constancy of the error terms (heteroscedasticity[16]). This is further supported by the Lagrange Multiplier (LM) test, which tests the null hypothesis H0 – no relationship between the variance of the error terms and estimates against H1 – there is a relationship between the variance of the error terms. H0 can generally be rejected if nR^2 is $> \chi_1^2$. Given that nR^2 is $< \chi_1^2$ H0 cannot be rejected and it can be concluded that there is no relationship between the variance of the error terms (Appendix 11a). Moreover, the Breusch-Pagan (BP) test at a 5% level of significance also shows no evidence for heteroscedasticity given that $Q < \chi_{p-1}^2$ (Appendix 11b).

Furthermore, the time series plot of the residuals and the run test for the regression model provides no graphical evidence that the regression assumption of independent error terms is violated (Appendix 12 and 13). This is further supported by the Durbin Watson d test, which does not provide evidence of autocorrelation[17], given that d lies within the zone of no positive and negative autocorrelation (Appendix 14). In addition, a simple t-test of the partial autocorrelation function, based on the hypothesis H0: there is no autocorrelation between the residuals against H1: there is autocorrelation between the residuals, indicates no relationship between the error terms. H0 can generally be rejected if either t $>$ 2.09302 or t $<$ - 2.09302.[18] The result of the partial autocorrelation function in Appendix 15 provides no evidence for first, second, third or fourth order autocorrelation, given that the t values of ET-3 (0.25) is $<$ 2.09 and ET-1 (-0.85), ET-2 (-0.94) and ET-4 (-0.92) are $>$ - 2.09 and H0 cannot be rejected respectively. Moreover, also the Ljung-Box Q (LBQ) statistic does not provide evidence of autocorrelation. The Ljung-Box Q statistic tests the null hy-

---

[16] Heteroscedasticity implies that the variance of the error terms is not constant and each of the error terms has its own distribution. This causes bigger variability in the error terms and the independent variable (LEV) and the hypothesis testing of the t and F statistics are consequently not reliable.

[17] The residuals do not oscillate from one side to another (oscillation i.e. negative autocorrelation).

[18] Student's t distribution with 19 DF: P(X <= x) = 0.9750 (5% level – two tailed); x = 2.09302.

pothesis, H0 – no k order autocorrelation against H1 – there is at least k order autocorrelation. H0 can be rejected if LBQk > χ_k^2. The test shows that LBQ1-4 is always < χ_{1-4}^2, given that (a) 0.81 < 3.84, (b) 1.51 < 5.99, (c) 1.87 < 7.81 and (d) 2.83 < 9.48 and H0 cannot be rejected for k = 1 to 4 respectively (Appendix 16). Consequently the Ljung-Box Q statistic provides additional evidence that no first, second, third or fourth order autocorrelation exists.

Another important assumption of the regression model is the independence of the explanatory variables with one another (multicollinearity[19]). The very low various inflation factors (VIFs) of the regression analysis in Appendix 5 indicate no significant multicollinearity, since all VIFs are < 10. On the other hand, the high pair wise correlation between the explanatory variables SIZE/PROF, SIZE/TANG, SIZE/VOL, PROF/VOL, GROPP/TANG and PROF/NDTS indicate that multicollinearity exists within the regression model. This is further supported by the regression of the explanatory variables against one another, which indicates multicollinearity especially for the variables PROF, SIZE and NDTS (Appendix 17).

5.4   Summary of empirical results and critique

The introduced statistical analysis on determinant of capital structure choice provides evidence consistent with both existing empirical studies and capital structure theory. Table (2) summarizes the findings of this analysis and compares them with the results of the previously discussed empirical studies.

---

[19] Multicollinearity describes a correlation between the explanatory variables with one another. It is an intrinsic problem of the regression model and could cause large variances in the slopes, including large standard deviations and standard errors and consequently high R2 and low t ratios, which distort the estimates of the regression parameters and statistical inferences (Dielman, 1996).

TABLE 2:

Summary of empirical studies of correlations between leverage and its explanatory variables

Variables	Titman & Wessels (1988)	Rajan & Zingales (1995)	Chen & Jiang (2001)	Drobetz & Fix (2003)	Friedrich & Co. (2004)
TANG	(+)/(-)[1]	(+)	(+)/(-)[1]	(+)	(+)
SIZE	(+)	(+)[2]	(+)	(+)	(+)
GROPP	(-)	(-)	(+)	(-)	(-)
PROF	(-)	(-)[2]	(-)	(-)	(+)
VOL	(-)	n.a.	(-)	(-)	(-)
NDTS	(+)/(-)	n.a.	(-)	n.a.	(-)

[1] Positively correlated with long term and negatively correlated with short term debt. [2] Except for Germany where size is negatively and profitability is positively correlated with leverage.

Particularly noteworthy and statistically significant is the high negative correlation between growth opportunities and leverage. The correlation coefficient of -0.708 suggests that firms with higher market-to-book ratios tend to have significantly lower levels of debt, which is consistent with both the trade-off and the pecking order theory. Furthermore, this evidence is consistent with the view that firms in growing industries are likely to have higher agency costs since they need more flexibility in their choice of future investments. This evidence also supports the view that high growth firms may find debt too costly, since they suffer the greatest loss when they have to pass up profitable investment opportunities. However, there may also be other potential reasons for the high negative correlation and firms with large market-to-book values may have a tendency to issue equity because of their high stock price which implies in itself a negative correlation between leverage and market-to-book ratio (Rajan and Zingales, 1995).

The second strongest and statistically reliable correlation is between size and leverage. The positive correlation coefficient of 0.568 suggests that larger firms tend to have higher levels of debt. Since larger firms tend to be more diversified and fail less often, they should have lower bankruptcy costs and the positive correlation between size and leverage is consistent with the trade-off theory. Furthermore, this result is in line with the creditor friendly German bankruptcy code, which is not conducive to restructuring firms and potential bankruptcy costs are expected to be higher due to a higher probability of liquidation in the case of financial distress. However, this evidence is contrary to the results reported in Rajan and Zingales (1995) which postulate that large firms in Germany have substantially less debt than small firms and size and leverage are negatively correlated.

The third strongest but statistically insignificant correlation is between tangibility and leverage. Nevertheless, given that tangibility is almost always positively correlated with leverage in the previously explored empirical studies, it could be assumed that the trade-off theory has some relevance in explaining leverage ratios for the German P&H industry. Furthermore, it is fairly obvious that the firm's debt capacity should increase in line with the proportion of tangible or collateralizable assets. Besides the statistically insignificant correlation between tangibility and leverage, there is also an insignificant positive correlation between profitability and leverage. The correlation coefficient of 0.322 suggests that more profitable firms tend to have more debt in capital structure which is in general consistent with the trade-off theory but contrasts sharply with what the pecking order theory suggests. However, this relationship is not supported by most of the introduced empirical studies as only Rajan and Zingales report a positive but also insignificant correlation between profitability and leverage for the German market. The negative relationship between leverage and volatility and leverage and non-debt tax shields is generally in line with the trade-off theory and the above examined empirical studies. Nevertheless one should be cautious in interpreting these results because the p-values of the correlation co-efficients indicate that they are all statistically insignificant.

However, a general critique of the introduced proxies of capital structure is that they could also measure other effects and therefore bias the statistical interpretation of the regression results. For example, firms with high depreciation, depletion and amortisation ratios are more likely to have higher proportions of tangible assets and fewer growth opportunities, since all of the three proxies are tied to the same denominator – total assets. This in turn implies a positive correlation between non-debt tax shields and leverage (Ozkan, 2001). However, the table of correlation coefficients in Appendix 7 does not confirm this relationship.

Besides the significance of some of the correlation coefficients, the regression model indicates that all of the introduced variables have some explanatory power since the goodness of fit ($R2$) does not improve when one or more of the explanatory variables are removed. Moreover, the analysis of the regression model assumptions outlines the practicality of the regression model in estimating leverage ratios for firms within the German P&H industry. The statistical investigation provides general evidence to conclude that heteroscedasticity and autocorrelation does not seem to exist within the regression model. However, it should be kept in mind that the introduced tests provide only general evidence supporting the conclusion that neither of these two assumptions is violated. Nevertheless, multicollinearity seems to exist between the explanatory variables which could distort the estimates of the regression model statistics and affect the validity of the regression model application. This leads to the general criticism of estimating a regression model with proxies for unobservable theoretical attributes.

As summarised by Titman and Wessels (1988), there may be no unique proxies for the theoretical attributes and choosing a single indicator may bias the interpretation of the statistical tests. Furthermore, it is often difficult to measure a particular attribute that is not related to other attributes in the regression model. This causes multicollinearity and could distort the estimates of the regression parameters and the statistical inferences. Moreover, since the observed variables are proxies of particular attributes and consequently imperfect representations of the theoretical attributes, their use in regression analysis introduces errors-in-variability problems, which could cause biased parameter estimates. Finally, measurement errors in the independent variables create spurious effects even when the unobserved attributes are not related to the dependent variable.

5.5 Analyzing the capital structure of Schwarz Pharma AG

After having introduced the industry analysis of capital structure, the following part investigates the capital structure of one firm out of the Prime Pharma and Healthcare Index more thoroughly.

Schwarz Pharma AG is a medium sized German pharmaceutical company principally active in the US, Europe and Germany. The company develops, manufactures and markets pharmaceuticals and specialises in the central nervous system, urology, and cardiovascular diseases. In the financial year 2003, Schwarz Pharma AG achieved sales of € 1,496 million and an EBITDA of € 335 million. Earnings per share (EPS) increased from € 1.1 to € 2.94, with a proposed dividend of € 0.60 per share. In 2003, the company reduced its total long term debt from € 95.45 to 69.82 million and increased its amount of cash and short term investments by approximately 29% to € 213 million. This results in a current negative Net Debt to Common Equity ratio (LEV) of about -0.24. Furthermore, Schwarz Pharma AG has a very low Total Debt to Total Asset ratio of about 0.08 and an interest cover of 28.96 times, which is exemplary (Schwarz Pharma AG Annual Report, 2003).

Even though Schwarz Pharma is a multinational corporation with a significant proportion of its operations outside Germany (85% of their sales are generated from international activities), it has a fairly domestic capital structure with a family share of 67% in the firm's total equity and a share of domestic bank loans in the firms total long term debt of about 83%. According to the annual report (2003), Schwarz Pharma has shareholders equity of € 577.026 million and long term debt of € 63.168 million. Total shareholders equity consists mainly of retained earnings (approximately 70%) and paid-in capital (approximately 26%). Total long term debt consists predominantly of unsecured bank loans, which all bear interest at fixed rates. In addition, the company has substantial amounts of undrawn domestic and foreign lines of credit agreements, totalling € 174.6 million as of the end of 2003.

The WACC is calculated by the weighted proportions of debt and equity capital multiplied by the appropriate rate of return. Empirical evidence of corporate practice shows that the CAPM is frequently used to calculate the required rate of return on equity capital. The CAPM relates the required rate of return for equity capital to the company's level of systematic risk and the average- and risk-free-rate of return in the market. Schwarz Pharma AG's cost of equity, based on the Bloomberg risk free rate of return for the Euro of 4.09 (Financial Times benchmark index for 10-Year German government bond yields is slightly less at 4.06), the market return of 10.72 and the adjusted beta for Schwarz Pharma AG of 1.07, could be estimated by using the CAPM at 11.18%.

$$(3) \qquad \overline{R}_{SP} = R_f + (\overline{R}_m - R_f) * \beta_{SP} \,^{20}$$

---

[20] $\overline{R}_{SP}$ = rate of return, R_f = risk free rate of return, $\overline{R}_m$ = average or index return on the market, β_{SP} = company risk in relation to the market risk.

The Theory of Capital Structure

$$11.18\% = 4.09\% + (10.72\% - 4.09\%)*1.07^{21}$$

[*Source: Bloomberg, (Appendix 20 and 22)]

The above undertaken calculation shows that Schwarz Pharma AG's shareholders should have a required rate of return of 11.18% for their equity
capital in relation to the company's level of systematic risk and the average
and risk free rate of return in the market. However, by using the DAX index
as a benchmark for the Beta coefficient, the calculation assumes that
Schwarz Pharma AGs shareholders are limited to a DAX portfolio and do
not invest or diversify in international stocks. Furthermore, by using the
Bloomberg base country data for the Euro as a proxy for the market portfolio and the risk free rate of return, the calculation assumes that Schwarz
Pharma AGs shareholders are limited to a European portfolio. These assumptions are fairly unrealistic and the calculations should rather be based
on world market figures which would alter the expected return, the risk free
rate and the beta factor of Schwarz Pharma AG and consequently the required cost of equity.

After having calculated the cost of equity, the WACC approach can be used
to calculate Schwarz Pharma AGs overall cost of capital as follows. As of
September 2004, Schwarz Pharma AG has Total Common Equity of
€ 577.026 million and total long and short term debt of € 76.870 million
(Schwarz Pharma AG Annual Report, 2003). Accordingly, about 88% of
the overall financing mix is equity and the remaining 12% is debt. Based on
the estimated cost of equity of 11.18% and the weighted average interest
rate of 4.5% and the corporate tax rate of 50.9%, as reported in the Annual
Report 2003, the cost of capital can be calculated at 10.11%.[22]

---

[21] R_f= 4.09 and $\overline{R}_m$ = 10.72 (Bloomberg base country data for the euro as at 03rd September
2004), β_{SP} = 1.07 (the regression of the monthly average volatility of Schwarz Pharma AG towards the DAX index shows a slightly lower unadjusted beta value of 0.523 compared to 0.67
as reported by the Bloomberg regression analysis in Appendix 21).
[22] K_0 = WACC, K_e = risk adjusted cost of equity, K_d = cost of debt before tax, V_e = market
value of equity, V_d = market value of debt, t_c = corporate tax rate, K_d (1- t_c) = the after-tax cost
of debt.

$$(2) \qquad K_{SP} = K_e \frac{V_e}{V_e + V_d} + K_d(1 - t_c)\frac{V_d}{V_e + V_d}$$

$$10.11\% = 11.18\%* 88\% + 4.5\%*51\%*12\%$$

The WACC calculation illustrates that Schwarz Pharma AG's average cost of capital is only slightly lower than its cost of equity capital. This is due to the fact that Schwarz Pharma AG does not use much debt financing even though their tax benefits from using debt are considerably high. Assuming that the above stated regression model could be used to estimate the optimal capital structure for any of the companies in the Prime Pharma and Health-care Index, the optimal Net Debt to Common Equity ratio could be estimated for Schwarz Pharma AG at 0.07. Accordingly, Schwarz Pharma AG should increase its total debt by approximately € 173 million from € 77 to € 253 million[23]. Assuming that the cost of equity and the cost of debt are unaffected by the changes in capital structure and that Total Common Equity as well as the amount of Cash and Short Term Investments remain unchanged, the proportion of debt in capital structure would increase to 30% and the weighted average cost of capital would decline to 8.51%.

As introduced in the beginning, the theory of enterprise evaluation postulates that the value of the company can be estimated by discounting the expected future cash flows at the firm's cost of capital. The market value of the firm or shareholder wealth can thereby be increased by decreasing the companies average cost of capital or by increasing the firm's future cash flows. The latter can be estimated as the earnings before interest, depreciation and amortisation reduced by the cash flows from financing and investment activities minus any increase in cash and cash equivalents (Arnold, 2002). Accordingly, Schwarz Pharma AG's cash flows can be calculated at

---

[23] (TotalDebt - Cash and ShortTermInvestment)/Total Common Equity = 0.07

€ 168.6 million[24]. Assuming that Schwarz Pharma AG's cash flows are expected to grow at 8% forever, the value of the firm could be estimated, with a simple discounted cash flow model, at € 1,768 million.

$$(13) \qquad V_{SP} = \frac{C_0(1+g)}{WACC - g}$$

$$€1,768 = \frac{€168.6 * 1.08}{10.11\% - 0.08}$$

Using the optimal capital structure as proposed by the regression model (12) and the WACC of 8.51%, Schwarz Pharma AG's firm value would increase by € 392 million to € 2,160. Although this illustration makes the choice of an optimal capital structure seem easy, there are some practical problems that arise from estimating capital structure and firm value by using the cost of capital approach.

Firstly, the cost of equity and cost of debt are estimated by the use of current data and the entire schedule of future financing costs is not available in advance. Secondly, the analysis is highly sensitive to its assumptions and any changes in the cash flow definition, market premium or the beta factor could change the estimated WACC and consequently the value of the company considerably. Thus, differences in data inputs mean that the WACC is a fairly subjective estimate for each firm. Thirdly, the analysis implicitly assumes that future cash flows are unaffected by the financing mix and the firm's financial risk and the required rate of return for debt and equity capital do not change. Furthermore, a mathematical constraint of the model is that the growth rate (g) cannot be greater than the average cost of equity, but over the long term this would not happen (Arnold, 2002). In general, the

---

[24] € 343.8 million - € 129.8 million - € 46.4 million = € 168.6 million (EBIDA – CF F&I – WC)

growth rate of the company should not significantly differ from the growth in nominal gross national product (real GNP plus inflation). Nevertheless, Schwarz Pharma operates in a highly innovative sector with a growth in sales of 35.6% compared to previous years so an average growth rate of 8% to infinity seems to be fairly realistic, even if the company predicts a significant decline in sales in 2004 (Schwarz Pharma AG Annual Report, 2003).

However, empirical evidence of corporate practice as carried out by Graham and Harvey (2001) or Bancel and Mittoo (2002) shows that companies use the capital asset pricing model to estimate their equity cost of capital. Furthermore, Rutterford and Gregory (1999) and Rutterford (2000) suggest that for the risk free rate of return most of the firms use government bond yields with maturities between 7 and 20 years. Beta values are taken from financial databases or professional advisors and the equity risk premium is estimated within a range of 4.5 to 6 per cent (Arnold, 2002). The above undertaken calculations are therefore very close to corporate practice and fairly realistic.

However, even if the market value of the firm can be theoretically optimized, shareholder wealth only increases when the market evaluates changes in capital structure efficiently. The difference between the current market capitalisation of Schwarz Pharma AG of about € 1,335 million and the estimated firm value of € 1,768 million shows that the model does not predict the market value of the firm correctly and might therefore be not as accurate as assumed. Besides the assumed optimum, which is significantly higher than the current level of debt, Schwarz Pharma AG reduced its total long term debt in 2003 by approximately 28% and moved away from its theoretical optimum as estimated by the regression model. A reason for this behaviour might be its very good performance in 2003 and the dismal sales prospects for the year 2004 which might also be anticipated by the market in the current market capitalisation of Schwarz Pharma AG.

In general, the debt to equity trade-off of Schwarz Pharma AG can be summarized as following. The tax benefits from using debt are significant, since the firm has a marginal tax rate of 51% and does not have very much depreciation, depletion and amortisation expenses. The benefits from using debt to add discipline to the management should be relatively small, since the CEO is a member of the Schwarz family and consequently one of the majority shareholders. Direct bankruptcy costs are probably small but indirect costs are likely to be substantial, especially as the company has substantial amounts of intangible assets. Agency costs of debt are likely to be high, given that the firm's fixed assets are relatively low compared to its total assets. Additionally, the firm has substantial amounts of intangible assets, which are difficult to liquidate and monitor during operations. Finally, flexibility needs for Schwarz Pharma are generally high, given that the firm operates in a highly innovative and competitive industry and further expansion and acquisitions are key aspects of their future strategy. In general, this seems to be the case for nearly all large German P&H companies and might be the main reason for the very low leverage ratios across this industry.

As a result, Schwarz Pharma AG seems to overemphasize financial flexibility and does not consider the substantial tax benefits of using debt. Even if the importance of bankruptcy costs tends to be large, there is generally upside potential for more debt in the firm's capital structure. For the management of the firm, this financial strategy might be beneficial but considering shareholder wealth, it would be better to use higher levels of debt than is currently being done by the company.

6   Summary of investigation and conclusion

Whether or not an optimal capital structure exists is one of the most important and complex issues in corporate finance. The traditional view argues
that an optimal capital structure exists and that it is determined by the gain
from using *"cheaper"* debt in relation to the costs of financial risk and the
higher required rate of return for debt capital. However, this approach assumes that future cash flows are always positively affected by the tax advantage of using debt and ignores the risk of increasing the variability of
earnings for shareholders.

In contrast, Modigliani and Miller (1958) provide the theoretical arguments
under which total firm value and its cost of capital are independent of capital structure. However, their conclusions are based on some unrealistic assumptions about reality and introducing some real world imperfections
changes the result of their model significantly. By relaxing the assumption
of no corporate taxes, an optimal capital structure seems to exist and is exactly where the level of debt is at its maximum. Introducing personal taxes
into the model of capital structure reduces the tax advantage of debt which
depends now on the relevant corporate and personal tax regulations and the
differential between corporate and personal tax rates. The existence of
bankruptcy costs further reduces the advantage of using debt, particularly
for highly levered firms, which consequently face higher bankruptcy costs
in the form of higher spreads on interest rates up front. When both taxes and
bankruptcy costs are considered, an optimal capital structure seems to exist
and is exactly where any additional gain from using debt is exactly offset by
the expected costs of bankruptcy. Optimal capital structure is thereby determined not only by trading off the benefits of debt against the risks and
costs of financial distress but also agency costs. Like bankruptcy costs,
agency costs are expected to increase at a comparative rate with leverage
and may therefore limit the amount of debt in capital structure. Furthermore, other issues in the context of agency costs such as the conflicts be-

tween shareholders and managers or debt holders and shareholders might affect the financing decision of the firm and limit the optimal amount of debt in capital structure.

In sharp contrast to the trade-off theory, the pecking order theory suggests that no optimal capital structure exists and that firms prefer to use their internal equity to finance their investment opportunities and favour debt over equity when external financing is needed. The pecking order theory is based on the arguments of information asymmetry and assumes that the information costs associated with external financing dominate all other considerations of the firm's financing decision. Furthermore, it assumes that managers possess better information about the firm than outsiders and that they tend to make their finance decision along these information asymmetries.

The investigated empirical evidence on the introduced capital structure theories provides no clear answer to the question of whether these theories are entirely useful in explaining corporate financing behaviour in practice. The statistical evidence on tax and bankruptcy costs however suggest that they are both significant in explaining the capital structure decision of firms in practice. This supports the practical relevance of the trade-off theory, which is further supported by the introduced evidence on target capital structures and industry related leverage ratios. On the other hand, the statistical evidence on the pecking order theory provides no clear or at least only moderate support that it is useful in explaining financing behaviour in practice.

Collectively, the empirical results of the statistical modelling techniques suggest that the trade-off and the pecking order theory are not mutually exclusive and are both useful in explaining debt policies in practice. However, capital structure is difficult to test statistically given that the theoretical attributes are not directly observable and that accounting measures are imperfect proxies. Furthermore, accounting measures are often related to one another which could distort the estimated parameters and the statistical inferences in statistical modelling approaches as in regression analysis.

Despite the cross sectional evidence on determinants of capital structure via regression and linear structural modelling techniques, the analysis of empirical surveys provides moderate support for the practical relevance of the trade-off theory but little evidence of the pecking order theory. Furthermore, the analysed studies reveal that informal criteria such as financial flexibility, credit rating or earnings per share dilution are the most important factors when mangers decide on their firm's debt policy.

The empirical part of this investigation uses multiple regression analysis to investigate determinants of capital structure choice for the German P&H industry. The analysis of correlation highlights two firm specific factors which specifically influence the firm's leverage decision - the proxies for growth opportunities and size. These results support the practical relevance of the trade-off theory but also provide moderate support for the pecking order theory. Furthermore, the results highlight the importance of financial flexibility and bankruptcy costs, which is also in line with the creditor friendly German bankruptcy code.

Additional evidence relating to the practical relevance of the trade-off theory is provided by the positive correlation between leverage and tangibility as well as leverage and profitability but one should be cautious when interpreting these results because the correlation coefficients p-values between these pairs are statistically insignificant.

The cross sectional regression result suggests that approximately 2/3 of the firm's leverage decision is explained by the regression model, but indicates that multicollinearity exists between the explanatory variables, which could affect the regression model statistics and the validity of the regression model application. Assuming that an industry optimum exists, the regression model (12) is adequate to estimate a target range of optimal capital structure for any firm within the German P&H industry. Furthermore, the analysis highlights some fundamental problems when using cross sectional regression analysis to estimate optimal capital structure on the basis of accounting indicators as proxies for the unobservable theoretical attributes.

The analysis of Schwarz Pharma AG's capital structure illustrates how the regression model could be used to determine the theoretical optimum of debt in capital structure and shows how the firm value of Schwarz Pharma AG could theoretically be increased by moving closer to the proposed industry optimum.

However, it remains an open question whether the introduced capital structure theories are sufficient enough to explain financing behaviour in practice and whether the introduced proxies of the determinants of capital structure capture the theoretical attributes entirely. Therefore, it is necessary to strengthen the relationship between theoretical models and empirical proxies which might be achieved with more detailed data and consequently more accurate proxies. It is likely that new capital structure theories will be developed in future which incorporate the investment opportunity set or the need for financial flexibility into the model of optimal capital structure, since they seem to be of utmost importance when managers and firms decide on their firm's debt policy.

BIBLIOGRAPHY

BOOKS

Arnold, G. (2002), *'Corporate Financial Management'*, 2nd ed. Harlow: Financial Times Prentice Hall, chap. 16, 17 & 18.

Bauer, W. (1998), *'Finanzierungstheorie: Eine Systematische Einführung'*, Wiesbaden: Gabler, pp. 80-120.

Brealey, R.A. and Myers S.C. (1996), *'Principles of Corporate finance'*, 5th ed. New York: McGraw-Hill, chap. 17, 18 & 19.

Copeland, T.E., Weston, K. and Shastri, K. (2004), *'Financial Theory and Corporate Policy'*, 4th ed. Boston: Pearson Addison-Wesley, chap. 15.

Damodaran, A. (2002), *'Corporate Finance – Theory and Practice'*, 2nd ed. New York: John Wiley & Sons, chap. 18, 19 & 20

Dielman, T. (1996), *'Applied regression analysis for business and economics'*, 2nd ed. Belmont, Calif.: Duxbury Press, chap. 3, 4, 5 & 6.

Eiteman, D.K., Stonehill, A.I. and Moffett, M.H. (2004), *'Multinational business finance'*, 9th ed. MA: Addison-Wesley Longman, chap. 11, 12, 13 & 14.

Nobes, C. (1996), *'Accounting comparisons: UK, Netherlands, France & Germany'*, London: Coopers & Lybrand, chap. 1, 2, 3 & 4.

Rutterford, J. (1988), *'An International Perspective on the Capital Structure Puzzle'*, in Stern, J.M. and Chew, D.H. (eds), *'New Developments in Corporate Finance'*, Oxford: Blackwell, pp. 194-207.

Samuels, J.M., Wilkes, F.M and Brayshaw R.E. (1996), *'Management of Company Finance'*, 6th ed. London: Chapman and Hall, chap. 18.

Van Horne, J.C. (1998), *'Financial Management and Policy'*, 11th ed. New Jersey: Prentice Hall, chap. 9 & 10.

ARTICLES AND JOURNALS

Altman, E. (1984), *'A Further Empirical Investigation of the Bankruptcy Cost Question'*, Journal of Finance, Vol. 39 (4), pp. 1067-1089, in Brealey and Myers (1996).

Asquith, P. and Mullins, D.W. (1983), *'The impact of initiating dividend payments on shareholder wealth'*, Journal of Business, Vol. 56, pp. 77-96.

Baker, M. and Wurgler, F. (2002), *'Market Timing and Capital Structure'*, Journal of Finance, Vol. 57 (1).

Bancel, F. and Mittoo, U. (2001), *'European managerial perceptions of the net benefits of foreign stock listings'*, European Financial Management Journal, Vol. 7 (2), pp. 213-236.

Barclay, M.J. and Smith, C.W. (1999), *'The Capital Structure Puzzle: Another Look at the Evidence'*, Journal of Applied Corporate Finance, Vol. 12 (1), pp. 8-20.

Booth, L., Aivazian, V., Demirguc-Kunt, A. and Maksimovic, V. (2001). *'Capital Structure in Developing Countries'*, Journal of Finance, Vol. 61 (1), in Bancel and Mittoo (2001).

Bowen, R.M., Daley, L.A. and Huber, C.C. (1982), *'Evidence on the existence and determinants of inter-industry differences in Leverage'*, Financial Management, Vol. 11 (4), pp. 10-20, in Harris and Raviv (1991).

Bowman, R. (1980), *'The importance of a market-value measurement of debt in assessing leverage'*, Journal of Accounting Research, Vol. 18(1), pp. 242-254, in Titman and Wessels (1988).

Bradley, M., Gregg, J.A. and Kim, H.E. (1984), *'On the existence of an optimal capital structure'*, Journal of Finance, Vol. 39, pp. 899-917.

Chaplinsky, S. and Niehaus, G. (1990), *'The Determinants of Inside Ownership and Leverage'*, University of Michigan Working Paper, in Harris and Raviv (1991).

Chirinko, R.S. and Singha, A.R. (2000), *'Testing static tradeoff against pecking order models of capital structure: a critical comment'*, Journal of Financial Economics, Vol. 58(3), pp. 417-425, in Copeland et al (2004).

Cordes, J.J. and Sheffrin, S.M. (1983), *'Estimating the tax advantage of corporate debt'* Journal of Finance, Vol. 38, pp. 95-105, in Copeland et al (2004).

DeAngelo, H. and Masulis, R. (1980), *'Optimal Capital Structure under Corporate and personal taxation'*, Journal of Financial Economics, Vol. 8, pp. 3-29.

DeBondt, G.J. (1998), *'Financial structure: theories and stylized facts for six EU Countries'*, De Economist, 146(2), pp. 271-301, in Chen and Jiang (2001).

Dietrich, R.J. (1984), '*Effects of Early Bond Refundings: An Empirical Investigation of Security Returns*', Journal of Accounting and Economics, Vol. 6, pp. 67-98, in Copeland et al (2004).

Donaldson, G. (1961), '*Corporate Debt Capacity*', Harvard: Harvard University Press, in Samuels et al (1996).

Eckbo, B.E. and Masulis, R.W. (1995), '*Seasoned equity offerings: A survey*', in Jarrow, R. et al., '*Handbooks in Operations Research and Management Science*', Vol. 9, New York: Elsevier Science, pp. 1017-1072.

Fama, E.F. (1978), '*The Effects of a Firm's Investment and Financing Decisions on the Welfare of Its Security Holders*', American Economic Review, Vol. 68(3), pp. 272-284.

Frank, M. and Goyal, V. (2003), '*Testing the Pecking Order Theory of Capital Structure*', Journal of Financial Economics, Vol. 67(2), pp. 217-48, in Copeland et al (2004).

Franks, J. and Mayer, C. (1994), '*The market for corporate control in Germany*', LBS Working Paper, in Rajan and Zingales (1995).

Galai, D. and Masulis, D. (1976), '*The Option Pricing Model and the Risk Factor of Stock*', Journal of Financial Economics, Vol. 6, pp. 53-82, in Titman and Wessels (1988).

Graham, J. (1996), '*Debt and the Marginal Tax Rate*', Journal of Financial Economics, Vol. 41, pp. 41-73, in Barclay and Smith (1999).

Graham, J. and Harvey, C. (2001), '*The theory and practice of corporate finance: evidence from the field*', Journal of Financial Economics, Vol. 60, pp. 187-243.

Grossman, S. and Hart, O. (1986), '*The Costs and Benefits of Ownership: A Theory of Vertical and Lateral Integration*', Journal of Political Economy, Vol. 94, pp. 691-719, in Titman and Wessels (1988).

Harris, M. and Raviv, A. (1991), '*The theory of capital structure*', Journal of Finance, Vol. 46, pp. 297-355.

Jensen, M.C. and Meckling, W. (1976), '*Theory of the firm: managerial behaviour, agency cost and ownership structure*', Journal of Financial Economics, Vol. 3, pp. 305-360.

Kaiser, K. (1994), '*Corporate restructuring & financial distress: An international view of bankruptcy laws and implications for corporations facing financial distress*', INSEAD Working Paper, in Rajan and Zingales (1995).

Kim, W.S. and Sorensen, E.H. (1986), '*Evidence on the Impact of the Agency Costs of Debt in Corporate Debt Policy*', Journal of Financial and Quantitative Analysis, Vol. 21, pp. 131-144, in Harris and Raviv (1991).

Long, M. and Malitz, I. (1985), '*The Investment-Financing Nexus: Some Empirical Evidence*', Midland Corporate Finance Journal, Vol. 3 (3), in Barclay and Smith (1999).

Mackie-Mason, J. (1990), '*Do Taxes Affect Corporate Financing Decisions?*', Journal of Finance, Vol. 45, pp. 1471-1494, in Copeland et al (2004).

Miller, M.H. (1977), '*Debt and Taxes*', Journal of Finance, Vol. 32, pp. 261-276, in Brealey and Myers (1996).

Minton, B.A. and Wruck, K.H. (2001), '*Financial conservatism: evidence on capital structure from low leverage firms*', The Ohio State University, M. Fisher College of Business Working Papers, in Copeland et al (2004).

Modigliani, F. and Miller, M.H. (1958), '*The Cost of Capital, Corporation Finance, and the Theory of Investment*', American Economic Review, Vol. 48 (3), pp. 261–97, in Culp (2003).

Myers, S.C. (1977), '*The determinants of corporate borrowing*', Journal of Financial Economics, Vol. 5, pp. 147-175.

Myers, S.C. (1984), '*The capital structure puzzle*', Journal of Finance, Vol. 39, pp. 572–592.

Myers, S.C. and Majluf S.N. (1984), '*Corporate financing and investment decisions when firms have information investors do not have*', Journal of Financial Economics, Vol. 13, pp. 187–221.

Ozkan, A. (2001), '*Determinants of Capital Structure and Adjustment to Long Run Target: Evidence from UK Company Panel Data*', Journal of Business Finance & Accounting, Vol. 28 (1&2), pp. 175-198.

Rajan, R.G. and Zingales L. (1995), '*What do we know about capital structure? Some evidence from international data*', Journal of Finance, Vol. 50, pp. 1421–1460.

Robichek, A.A. and Myers, S.C. (1966), '*Conceptual problems in the use of risk-adjusted discount rates*', Journal of Finance, Vol. 21 (4), pp. 727-730.

Ross, S. (1977). '*The determination of financial structure: the incentive-signalling approach*', Bell Journal of Economics, Vol. 8, pp. 23–40, in Arnold (2002).

Rutherford, J. (1988), '*An international perspective on the capital structure puzzle*', in Stern, M.J. and Chew, D.H. (1988), '*New Developments in International Finance*', New York: Basil Blackwell.

Rutterford, J. (2000), '*The cost of capital and shareholder value*', in Arnold, G.C. and Davies, M. (2000), '*Value based management*', London: Wiley, in Arnold (2000).

Rutterford, J. and Gregory, A. (1999) '*The Cost of Capital in the UK: a comparison of the perceptions of industry and the city*', London: Chartered Institute of Management Accountants, in Arnold (2002).

Schwartz, E. and Aronson, R.J. (1967), '*Some Surrogate Evidence In Support of Optimal Financial Structure*', Journal of Finance, Vol. 22 (1), in Barclay and Smith (1999).

Shyam-Sunder, L. and Myers, S.C. (1999), '*Testing static tradeoff against pecking order models of capital structure*'. Journal of Financial Economics, Vol. 51, pp. 219-244, in Copeland et al (2004).

Smith, C. (1986), '*Investment Banking and the Capital Acquisition Process*' Journal of Financial Economics, Vol. 15, pp. 3-29, in Barclay and Smith (1999).

Titman, S. and Wessels, R. (1988), '*The determinants of capital structure choice*', Journal of Finance, Vol. 43, pp. 1-19.

Warner, J.B. (1977), '*Bankruptcy costs: some evidence*', Journal of Finance, Vol. 26, pp. 337-48, in Samuels et al (1996).

Weiss, L. (1990), '*Bankruptcy Resolution: Direct Costs and Violation of Priority of Claims*', Journal of Financial Economics, Vol. 27, pp. 285-314, in Brealey and Myers (1996).

White, M.J. (1993), '*Corporate bankruptcy: A U.S.-European comparison*', University of Michigan Working Paper, in Rajan and Zingales (1995).

Williamson, M. and Francis, S. (2001), '*The importance of optimal capital structure*', London: Euromoney, Iss. 391, p. 2.

INTERNET SOURCES

Bitz, M. (2000), '*Grundzüge der Theorie der Kapitalstruktur*'. Diskussionsbeitrag Nr. 295, Lehrstuhl für Betriebswirtschaftslehre, Fern-Universität Hagen. Available from: <http://www.econbiz.de/archiv/ha/fuha/bank/kapitalstruktur.pdf>. Accessed 15th July 2004.

Culp, C.L. (2003), '*The Modigliani-Miller Propositions*'. CP Risk Management LLC, The University of Chicago. Available from: <http://gsbwww.uchicago.edu/fac/christopher.culp/research/HORM-MM.pdf>. Accessed 18th July 2004.

Chen, L.H. and Jiang, G.J. (2001), '*The Determinants of Dutch Capital Structure Choice*'. Faculty of Business and Economics, University of Groningen. Available from: <http://www.ub.rug.nl/eldoc/som/e/01E55/01e55.pdf>. Accessed 18th July 2004.

Drobetz, W. and Fix, R. (2003), '*What are the determinants of the capital structure? Some evidence for Switzerland*', WWZ/Department of Finance Working Paper, University of Basel. Available from: <http://www.wwz.unibas.ch/cofi/publications/papers/2003/04-03.pdf>. Accessed 18th July 2004.

Schwarz Pharma Annual Report 2003. Available from: <http://www.schwarpharma.com/_uploads/assets/3348_Annual%20Report%20final%20%28long%29.pdf.>. Accessed 31th August 2004.

ELECTRONIC SOURCES

MINITAB Statistical Software, MINITAB release 13.1. Including: Regression analysis, tutorials and help functions.

BLOOMBERG PROFESSIONAL, Including: Beta factors and market data.

THOMSON FINANCIAL, Including: Datastream, Thomson Financial and Worldscope Databases

APPENDIX

1. Variable definition
2. Pharma and Healthcare Industry - data set
3. Initial regression model (LEV I – Net Debt/ Common Equity)
4. Graphical analysis and statistical testing for model improvements
5. Final regression model
6. Summary statistics
7. Table of correlations
8. Selected plots of the depended against the independent variables
9. Summary statistics – plots
10. Normality tests for residuals
11. Lagrange Multiplier (LM) and the Breusch-Pagan (BP) test for heteroscedasticity
12. Time series plots
13. Run test
14. Durbin Watson d test
15. Selected regression analysis' of explanatory of variables
16. Partial autocorrelation function
17. Ljung-Box statistic
18. Final regression model II (LEV II – Total Debt to Total Assets)
19. Table of correlations (LEV II – Total Debt to Total Assets)
20. Historical beta of Schwarz Pharma AG
21. Beta regression model Schwarz Pharma AG versus Dax
22. Base country data for Europe

1. Variable definition

LEV	–	Leverage; Net Debt to Common Equity
TANG	–	Tangibility; Ratio of Total Property Plant Equipment Gross to Total Assets
SIZE	–	Size; Natural Logarithm of Sales
GROPP	–	Growth opportunities; Ratio of Market Capitalisation to Total Assets
PROF	–	Profitability; Ratio of Earnings before Interest Taxes and Deprecation to Total Assets
VOL	–	Volatility; Variability of Sales 5Yr Moving Average
NDTS	–	Non debt tax shields; Ratio of Depreciation Depletion Amortisation Expense to Total Assets

2. Pharma and Healthcare Industry - data set

Companies	LEV	TANG	SIZE	GROPP	PROF	VOL	NDTS
IAS							
MERCK KGAA	0,63	0,62	3,86	0,31	9,58	0,27	0,069
AAP IMPLANTATE AG	1,64	0,49	1,04	1,00	-108,06	0,50	0,139
ALTANA AG	-0,33	0,52	3,44	2,62	25,61	0,32	0,050
BIOTEST AG	1,48	0,69	2,35	0,13	-5,45	0,21	0,031
CURASAN AG	-0,25	0,21	1,17	0,84	18,87	0,39	0,070
GERATHERM MEDICAL AG	-0,46	0,40	0,87	1,62	9,74	0,33	0,030
MEDIGENE AG	-0,61	0,19	0,00	2,12	-70,07	2,65	0,033
MORPHOSYS AG	-0,76	0,13	1,18	2,40	-16,33	0,55	0,054
MWG BIOTECH AG	-0,09	0,58	1,63	0,48	-28,29	0,30	0,114
NOVEMBER AG	-0,45	0,20	0,65	1,87	-10,70	0,28	0,032
PLASMASELECT AG	0,00	0,30	1,49	0,55	2,42	0,60	0,017
RHOEN-KLINIKUM AG	0,44	0,96	2,98	0,65	15,95	0,40	0,045
SCHERING AG	-0,22	0,64	3,68	1,67	15,18	0,11	0,056
STADA ARZNEIMITTEL AG	0,06	0,12	2,87	0,96	9,36	0,40	0,033
STRATEC BIOMED. SYS. AG	0,33	0,31	1,50	1,63	14,01	0,45	0,040
UMS UNITED MED. SYS. INT	1,80	0,67	1,80	0,25	-10,28	0,59	0,141
US-GAAP							
BIOLITEC AG	-0,21	0,30	1,26	1,23	-8,88	0,25	0,035
CARL ZEISS MEDITEC AG	-0,13	0,25	2,37	1,50	9,92	1,03	0,030
CYBIO AG	-0,25	0,41	1,08	0,82	-64,13	0,23	0,213
EVOTEC OAI AG	-0,03	0,43	1,89	0,44	-7,75	0,69	0,093
FRESENIUS AG	1,89	0,38	3,85	0,15	7,32	0,34	0,039
FRESENIUS MED. CARE AG	0,78	0,27	3,69	0,71	11,05	0,27	0,032
GIRINDUS AG	-0,22	0,63	1,50	0,53	-10,02	0,68	0,062
GPC BIOTECH AG	-1,09	0,09	1,33	2,22	-26,68	0,43	0,024
PULSION MEDICAL SYS. AG	-0,35	0,38	1,14	1,92	-9,11	0,36	0,066
SCHWARZ PHARMA AG	-0,24	0,32	3,18	1,40	23,93	0,44	0,056
WORLD OF MEDICINE AG	0,14	0,30	1,50	0,72	-13,84	0,25	0,068
WAVELIGHT LASER TECH. AG	0,54	0,12	1,68	1,08	6,45	0,75	0,032

3. Initial regression model (LEV I – Net Debt/Common Equity)

Regression Analysis: LEV versus TANG; SIZE; GROPP; PROF; VOL; NDTS

The regression equation is

```
LEV = 0,298 + 0,302 TANG + 0,272 SIZE - 0,619 GROPP -
0,0104 PROF - 0,055 VOL - 2,51 NDTS
```

Predictor	Coef	SE Coef	T	P	VIF
Constant	0,2982	0,5310	0,56	0,580	
TANG	0,3015	0,6306	0,48	0,637	1,5
SIZE	0,2723	0,1396	1,95	0,065	1,9
GROPP	-0,6190	0,1762	-3,51	0,002	1,4
PROF	-0,010356	0,005827	-1,78	0,090	2,6
VOL	-0,0551	0,2855	-0,19	0,849	1,5
NDTS	-2,511	3,607	-0,70	0,494	2,1

S = 0,565247   R-Sq = 57,7%   R-Sq(adj) = 45,6%

Analysis of Variance

Source	DF	SS	MS	F	P
Regression	6	9,1549	1,5258	4,78	0,003
Residual Error	21	6,7096	0,3195		
Total	27	15,8645			

Source	DF	Seq SS
TANG	1	2,8260
SIZE	1	0,8987
GROPP	1	4,2882
PROF	1	0,9858
VOL	1	0,0015
NDTS	1	0,1548

Unusual Observations

Obs	TANG	LEV	Fit	SE Fit	Residual	St Resid
2	0,490	1,640	0,853	0,432	0,787	2,16R
7	0,190	-0,610	-0,460	0,521	-0,150	-0,68X
16	0,670	1,800	0,556	0,310	1,244	2,63R

R denotes an observation with a large standardized residual. X denotes an observation whose X value gives it large influence.

Durbin-Watson statistic = 1,68751

4. Graphical analysis and statistical testing for model improvements

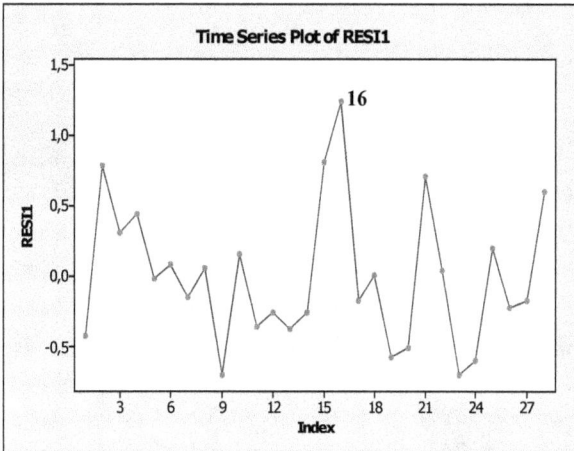

FIGURE 7 Time series plot HI1

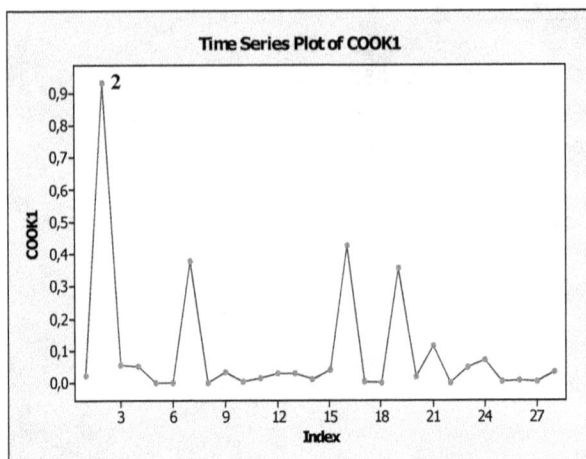

FIGURE 8 Time series plot COOK1

Regression Analysis: LEV versus TANG; SIZE; ...

The regression equation is

LEV = 0,489 − 0,032 TANG + 0,248 SIZE − 0,584 GROPP − 0,00409 PROF − 0,039 VOL − 4,74 NDTS + 1,73 d1 + 1,68 d2

Predictor	Coef	SE Coef	T	P	VIF
Constant	0,4894	0,3917	1,25	0,227	
TANG	−0,0325	0,4678	−0,07	0,945	1,5
SIZE	0,2480	0,1084	2,29	0,034	2,1
GROPP	−0,5842	0,1303	−4,48	0,000	1,4
PROF	−0,004089	0,006306	−0,65	0,524	5,7
VOL	−0,0386	0,2327	−0,17	0,870	1,8
NDTS	−4,743	2,998	−1,58	0,130	2,7
d1	**1,7296**	**0,6428**	**2,69**	**0,014**	**2,3**
d2	**1,6816**	**0,4963**	**3,39**	**0,003**	**1,4**

S = 0,413935   R-Sq = 79,5%   R-Sq(adj) = 70,8%

The test for the significance of the indicator variables shows that:

− Observation 2 (d1) is not influential in explaining the variation of the explanatory variable[25].
− Observation 16 (d2) is not influential in explaining the variation of the explanatory variable[26].

Analysis of Variance

Source	DF	SS	MS	F	P
Regression	8	12,6090	1,5761	9,20	0,000
Residual Error	19	3,2555	0,1713		
Total	27	15,8645			

Unusual Observations

Obs	TANG	LEV	Fit	SE Fit	Residual	St Resid
2	0,490	1,6400	1,6400	0,4139	0,0000	* X
16	0,670	1,8000	1,8000	0,4139	-0,0000	* X
21	0,380	1,8900	1,1161	0,2176	0,7739	2,20R

---

[25] The test for the significance of the indicator variables using the t and the p value of the dummies shows that H0 cannot be rejected for d1, given that 2,69 is > 2,0738 and 0,014 < 0,05 (Student's t distribution with 22 DF: $P(X <= x) = 0.9750$; x = 2,07387).Consequently it could be assumed that observation 2 (d1) is not influential in explaining the variation of the explanatory variable.
[26] H0 cannot be rejected for d2, given that 3,39 is > 2,0738 and 0,004 < 0,05 and it could be assumed that observation 16 (d2) is not influential in explaining the variation of the explanatory variable.

5. Final regression model

Regression Analysis: LEV versus TANG; SIZE; GROPP; PROF; VOL; NDTS

The regression equation is

```
LEV = 0,489 - 0,032 TANG + 0,248 SIZE - 0,584 GROPP -
0,00409 PROF - 0,039 VOL - 4,74 NDTS
```

Predictor	Coef	SE Coef	T	P	VIF
Constant	0,4894	0,3917	1,25	0,227	
TANG	-0,0325	0,4678	-0,07	0,945	1,4
SIZE	0,2480	0,1084	2,29	0,034	2,1
GROPP	-0,5842	0,1303	-4,48	0,000	1,3
PROF	-0,004089	0,006306	-0,65	0,524	3,2
VOL	-0,0386	0,2327	-0,17	0,870	1,8
NDTS	-4,743	2,998	-1,58	0,130	2,0

```
S = 0,413935   R-Sq = 69,0%   R-Sq(adj) = 59,2%
```

Analysis of Variance

Source	DF	SS	MS	F	P
Regression	6	7,2485	1,2081	7,05	0,000
Residual Error	19	3,2555	0,1713		
Total	25	10,5040			

Source	DF	Seq SS
TANG	1	1,2680
SIZE	1	2,2884
GROPP	1	3,1740
PROF	1	0,0085
VOL	1	0,0804
NDTS	1	0,4290

Unusual Observations

Obs	TANG	LEV	Fit	SE Fit	Residual	St Resid
6	0,190	-0,6100	-0,7276	0,3892	0,1176	0,83 X
19	0,380	1,8900	1,1161	0,2176	0,7739	2,20R

R denotes an observation with a large standardized residual. X denotes an observation whose X value gives it large influence.

Durbin-Watson statistic = 2,24577

6. Summary statistics

Descriptive Statistics: LEV; TANG; SIZE; GROPP; PROF; VOL; NDTS

Variable	Mean	SE Mean	StDev	Minimum
LEV	0,0231	0,127	0,648	-1,090
TANG	0,3750	0,0415	0,2116	0,0900
SIZE	2,005	0,216	1,101	0,000000000
GROPP	1,176	0,142	0,725	0,130
PROF	-3,53	4,64	23,66	-70,07
VOL	0,4992	0,0947	0,4827	0,1100
NDTS	0,05477	0,00769	0,03921	0,01700

Variable	Q1	Median	Q3	Maximum
LEV	-0,335	-0,170	0,358	1,890
TANG	0,2075	0,3150	0,5350	0,9600
SIZE	1,178	1,565	3,030	3,860
GROPP	0,545	1,020	1,720	2,620
PROF	-11,49	4,44	11,79	25,61
VOL	0,2700	0,3750	0,5625	2,6500
NDTS	0,03200	0,04250	0,06650	0,21300

7. Table of correlations

Correlations: LEV; TANG; SIZE; GROPP; PROF; VOL; NDTS

	LEV	TANG	SIZE	GROPP	PROF	VOL
TANG	0,347					
	0,082					
SIZE	**0,568**	**0,412**				
	0,002	**0,037**				
GROPP	**-0,708**	**-0,411**	-0,309			
	0,000	**0,037**	0,125			
PROF	0,322	0,185	**0,633**	-0,089		
	0,109	0,367	**0,001**	0,666		
VOL	-0,238	-0,279	**-0,404**	0,257	**-0,479**	
	0,243	0,167	**0,041**	0,205	**0,013**	
NDTS	-0,114	0,224	-0,114	-0,226	**-0,469**	-0,190
	0,578	0,272	0,580	0,268	**0,016**	0,351

Cell Contents: Pearson correlation
                   P-Value

8. Selected plots of the depended against the independent variables

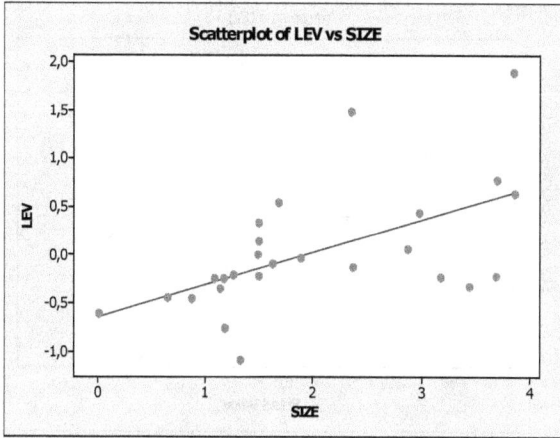

FIGURE 3 Scatter plot of LEV vs. GROPP

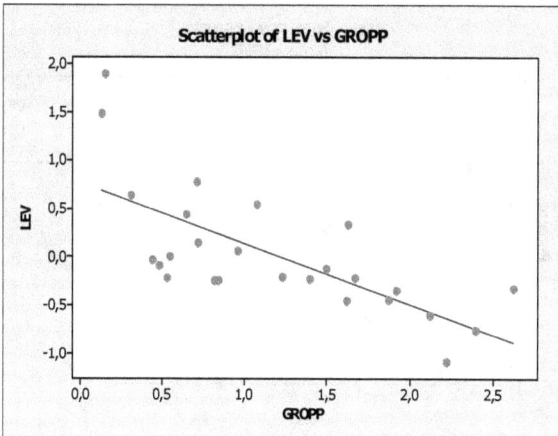

FIGURE 4 Scatter plot of LEV vs. SIZE

9. Summary statistics - plots

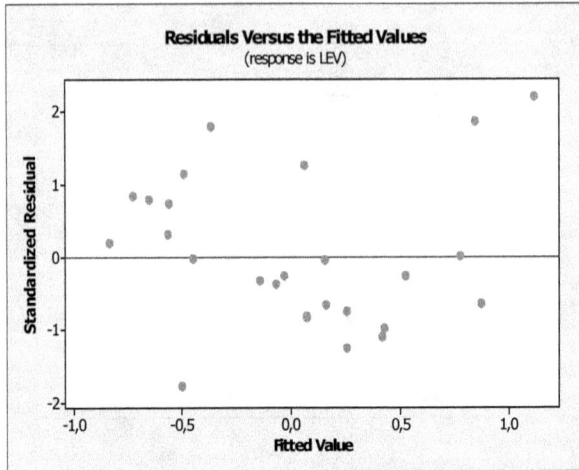

FIGURE 5 Scatter plot standardised residuals versus fitted values

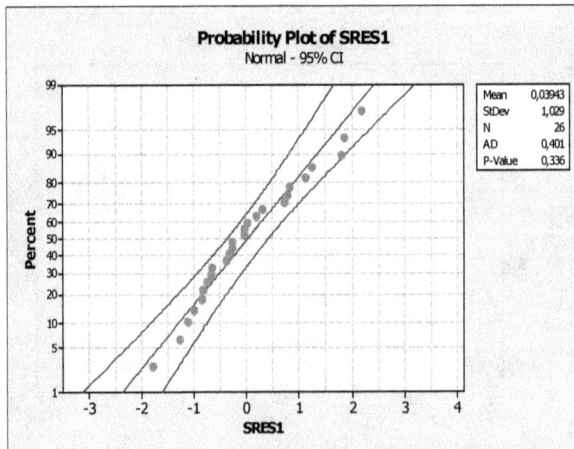

FIGURE 6 Normal probability plot of the residuals

10. Normality tests for residuals

a) Kolmogorov-Smirnov normality test

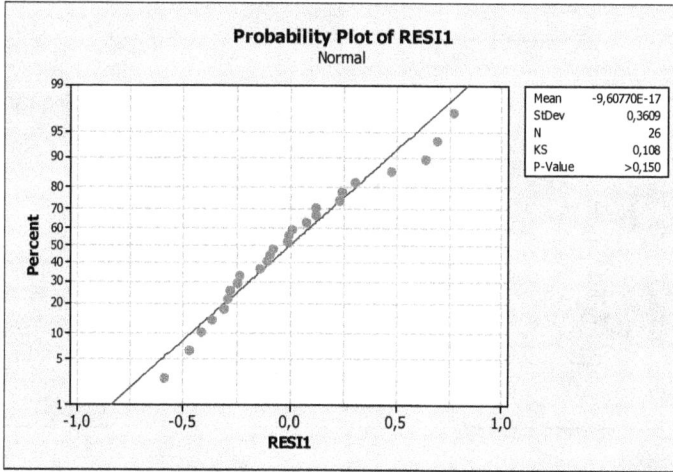

b) Ryan-Joiner (Similar to Sharpiro-Wilk) test for normality

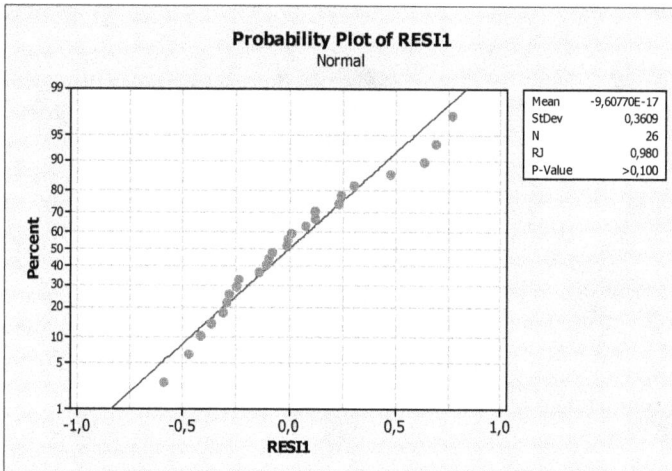

c) Anderson-Darling normality test

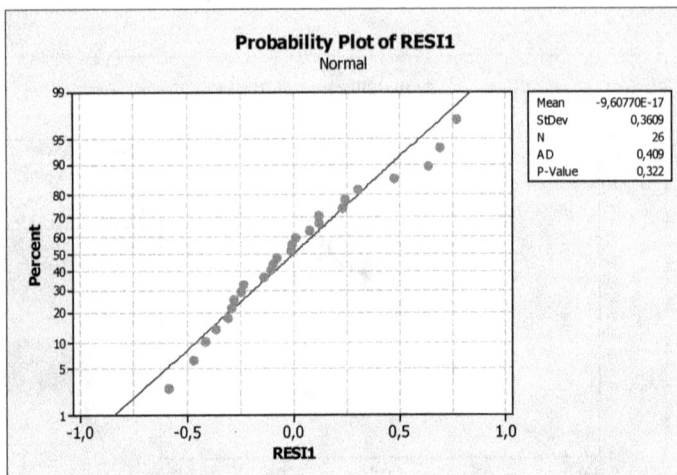

Probability Plot of RESI1
Normal

Mean	-9,60770E-17
StDev	0,3609
N	26
AD	0,409
P-Value	0,322

11. Lagrange Multiplier (LM) and the Breusch-Pagan (BP) test for heteroscedasticity

a) Lagrange Multiplier (LM) test

The LM test analyses whether any relationship exists between the variances of the error terms and the forecast. The hypothesis test can be stated as, H0 – no relationship between the variance of the error terms and estimates i.e. no heteroscedasticity and H1 – there is a relationship between the variance of the error terms i.e. heteroscedasticity. H0 can generally be rejected if nR^2 is $> \chi_1^2$. R2 is thereby obtained by regressing the squared residuals against the squared fits[27]. The result of the calculations shows a R2 of about 14.5% and nR2 can be calculated at 3.77.[28] Given that 3.77 is < 3.8415[29], H0 cannot be rejected and the LM test at a 5% level of significance provides no evidence for heteroscedasticity.

---

[27] SQRES = 0.0695 + 0.199 SQFITS; Regression results: S = 0.153897 R-Sq = 14.5% R-Sq(adj) = 10.9%
[28] 26*0.145 = 3.77
[29] Chi-Square with 1 DF: P(X <= x) = 0.9500; x = 3.8415

b) Breusch-Pagan (BP) test

The BP test analyses the underlying assumption that the errors in the original equation are normally distributed and that the variances depend upon a combination of the explanatory variables. It analyses the hypothesis $H_0 : \alpha_2 = \alpha_3 = \alpha_p = 0$ i.e. there is no heteroscedasticity against H1: at least one α_p is not equal to 0 i.e. there is heteroscedasticity. The null hypothesis can be rejected at the α% significance level if $Q > \chi^2_{p-1}$.

Q represents half of the error sum of squares and is obtained by regressing the previously computed G^{30} values against the explanatory variables. Given that 4.001 is $< 12.5916^{31}$ the BP test shows no evidence for heteroscedasticity and H0 cannot be rejected at a 5% level of significance.

---

[30] The values of the G variables are obtained by dividing the squared residuals by K1 (0.125212), which is the sum of squared residuals divided through the number of observations.
[31] ESS = 8.002, Q = 2.001 (8.002/2), Chi-Square with 6 DF: P(X <= x) = 0.9500; x = 12.5916.

12. Time series plots

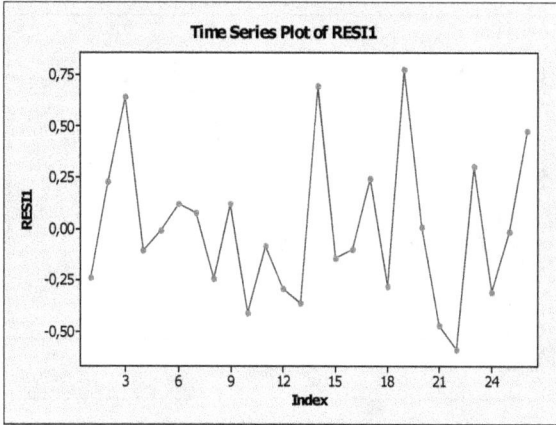

FIGURE 7 Time series plot residuals

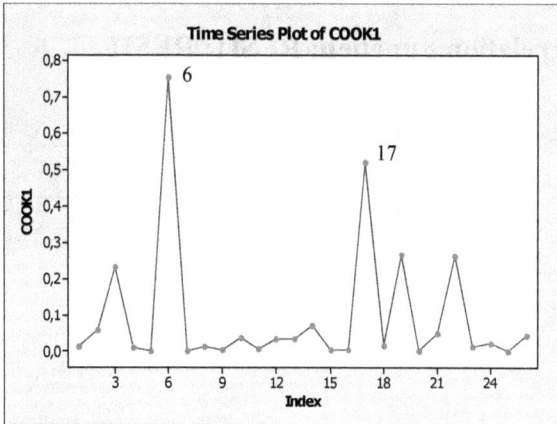

FIGURE 8 Time series plot COOK1

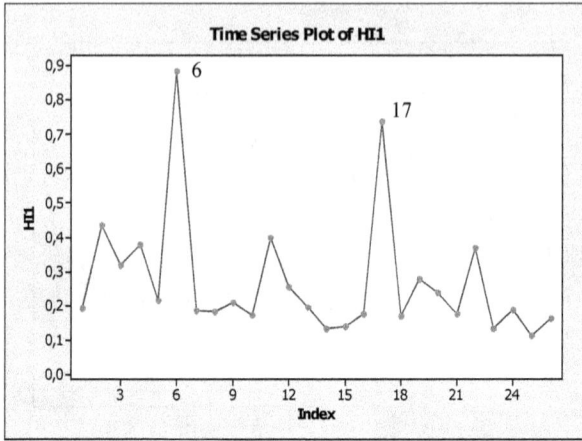

FIGURE 9 Time series plot HI1

13. Run test

Cross Correlation Function: RESI1; RESI1

```
CCF - correlates RESI1(t) and RESI1(t+k)


            -1.0 -0.8 -0.6 -0.4 -0.2  0.0  0.2  0.4  0.6
            +----+----+----+----+----+----+----+----+--
-15  -0,131                            XXXX
-14   0,100                            XXX
-13  -0,128                            XXXX
-12   0,238                            XXXXXXX
-11   0,139                            XXXX
-10  -0,107                            XXXX
 -9   0,065                            XXX
 -8  -0,108                            XXXX
 -7  -0,128                            XXXX
 -6  -0,031                            XX
```

Cross Correlation Function: RESI1; RESI1

```
CCF - correlates RESI1(t) and RESI1(t+k)

             -1.0 -0.8 -0.6 -0.4 -0.2  0.0  0.2  0.4  0.6
             +----+----+----+----+----+----+----+----+--
 -5  -0,013                                X
 -4  -0,171                              XXXXX
 -3   0,106                                XXXX
 -2  -0,152                              XXXXX
 -1  -0,166                              XXXXX
  0   1,000                                XXXXXXXXXXXXXXXX
  1  -0,166                              XXXXX
  2  -0,152                              XXXXX
  3   0,106                                XXXX
  4  -0,171                              XXXXX
  5  -0,013                                X
  6  -0,031                               XX
  7  -0,128                              XXXX
  8  -0,108                              XXXX
  9   0,065                                XXX
 10  -0,107                              XXXX
 11   0,139                                XXXX
 12   0,238                                XXXXXXX
 13  -0,128                              XXXX
 14   0,100                                XXX
 15  -0,131                              XXXX
```

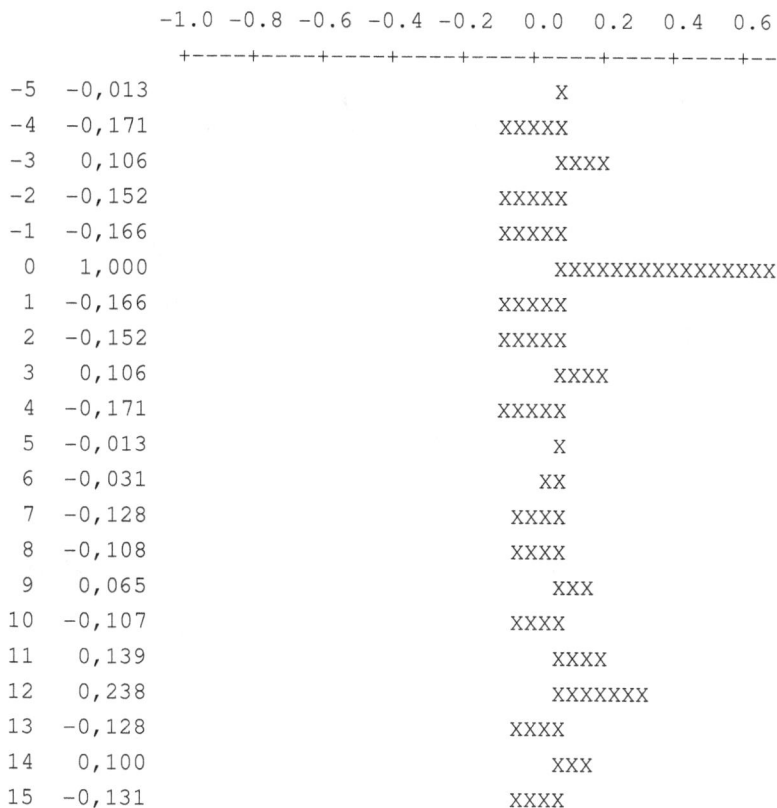

14. Durbin Watson d test[32]

Durbin Watson d Test: Decision Rules

Null Hypothesis	Decision	If
No + autocorrelation	Reject Ho	$0 < d < d_L$
No + autocorrelation.	No decision	$d_L \leq d \leq d_u$
No - autocorrelation.	Reject Ho	$4 - d_L < d < 4$
No - autocorrelation.	No Decision	$4 - d_u \leq d \leq 4 - d_L$
No +ve or -ve autocorrelation	**Do not reject Ho**	$d_u < d < 4 - d_u$

Applicable
$0 < 2.24 < 0{,}769$ (No)
$0{,}769 \leq 2{,}24 \leq 1{,}910$ (No)
$3{,}231 < 2{,}24 < 4$ (No)
$1{,}910 \leq 2{,}24 \leq 3{,}231$ (No)
$2{,}090 < 2{,}24 > 1{,}910$ (Yes)

- with n = 22 (number of observations), k`= 6 (number of explanatory variables) d = 2,24, dL = 0,769, 4- dL = 3,231, du = 2,090 and 4-du = 1,910

---

[32] The hypothesis test of the Durbin Watson analysis whether H0: there is no autocorrelation between the residuals against H1: there is autocorrelation between the residuals.

15. Selected regression analysis' of explanatory of variables (Multicollinearity)

Regression Analysis: PROF versus TANG; SIZE; GROPP; VOL; NDTS

The regression equation is

```
PROF = 2,3 + 3,3 TANG + 8,86 SIZE + 1,43 GROPP - 20,1
VOL - 300 NDTS
```

S = **14,6787**   R-Sq = **69,2%**   R-Sq(adj) = **61,5%**

Analysis of Variance

Source	DF	SS	MS	F	P
Regression	5	9687,0	1937,4	**8,99**	**0,000**
Residual Error	20	4309,3	215,5		
Total	25	13996,3			

Regression Analysis: SIZE versus TANG; GROPP; PROF; VOL; NDTS

The regression equation is
```
SIZE = 1,75 + 1,12 TANG - 0,219 GROPP + 0,0300 PROF +
0,053 VOL + 3,15 NDTS
```

```
S = 0,854041   R-Sq = 51,9%   R-Sq(adj) = 39,8%
```

Analysis of Variance

Source	DF	SS	MS	F	P
Regression	5	15,7195	3,1439	**4,31**	**0,008**
Residual Error	20	14,5877	0,7294		
Total	25	30,3072			

Regression Analysis: NDTS versus TANG; SIZE; GROPP; PROF; VOL

The regression equation is
```
NDTS = 0,0539 + 0,0304 TANG + 0,00412 SIZE - 0,00405
GROPP - 0,00133 PROF
      - 0,0376 VOL
```

```
S = 0,0308760   R-Sq = 50,4%   R-Sq(adj) = 38,0%
```

Analysis of Variance

Source	DF	SS	MS	F	P
Regression	5	0,0193761	0,0038752	**4,06**	**0,010**
Residual Error	20	0,0190665	0,0009533		
Total	25	0,0384426			

16. Partial Autocorrelation Function: RESI1

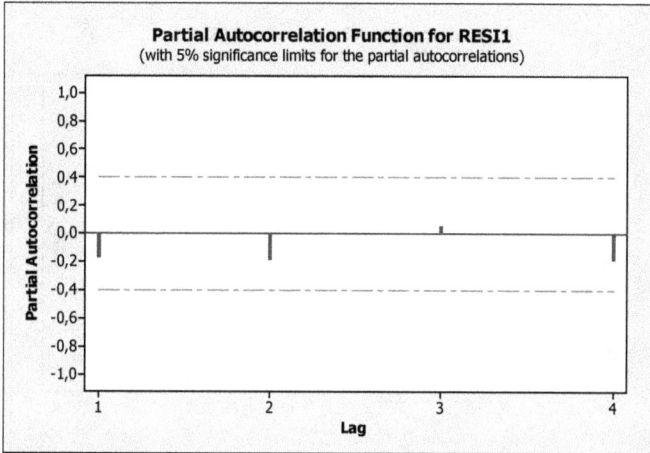

Partial Autocorrelation Function for RESI1
(with 5% significance limits for the partial autocorrelations)

Partial Autocorrelation Function: RESI1

Lag	PACF	T
1	-0,166405	-0,85
2	-0,185307	-0,94
3	0,048222	0,25
4	-0,180819	-0,92

17. Ljung-Box statistic

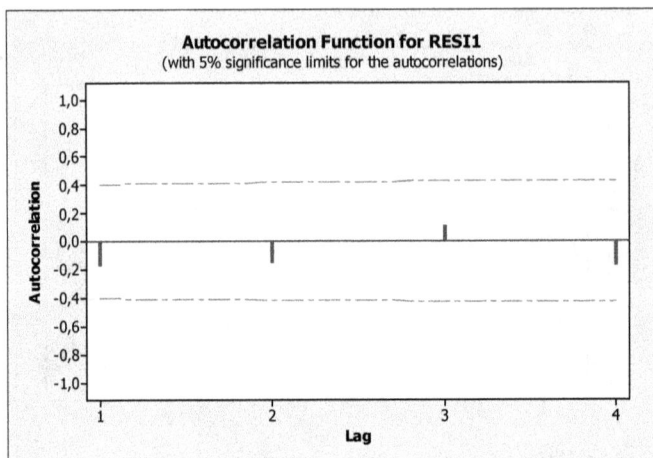

Autocorrelation Function for RESI1
(with 5% significance limits for the autocorrelations)

Autocorrelation Function: RESI1

```
Lag        ACF       T     LBQ        Chi-Square
  1  -0,166405  -0,85    0,81    <    3,84146  (1 DF&P=0.95)
  2  -0,152485  -0,76    1,51    <    5.99146  (2 DF&P=0.95)
  3   0,106189   0,52    1,87    <    7.81473  (3 DF&P=0.95)
  4  -0,170594  -0,82    2,83    <    9,48773  (4 DF&P=0.95)
```

18. Final regression model (LEV II – Total Debt to Total Assets)

Regression Analysis: LEV II versus TANG; SIZE; GROPP; PROF; VOL; NDTS

The regression equation is

```
LEV II = 0,293 + 0,0382 TANG + 0,0342 SIZE - 0,121 GROPP
 - 0,00107 PROF + 0,0163 VOL - 1,75 NDTS
```

Predictor	Coef	SE Coef	T	P	VIF
Constant	0,29257	0,07753	3,77	0,001	
TANG	0,03824	0,09259	0,41	0,684	1,4
SIZE	0,03418	0,02145	1,59	0,128	2,1
GROPP	-0,12057	0,02579	-4,68	0,000	1,3
PROF	-0,001073	0,001248	-0,86	0,401	3,2
VOL	0,01628	0,04605	0,35	0,728	1,8
NDTS	-1,7527	0,5934	-2,95	0,008	2,0

S = 0,0819333   R-Sq = 69,3%   R-Sq(adj) = 59,5%

Analysis of Variance

Source	DF	SS	MS	F	P
Regression	6	0,287348	0,047891	7,13	0,000
Residual Error	19	0,127548	0,006713		
Total	25	0,414896			

Unusual Observations

Obs	TANG	LEV	Fit	SE Fit	Residual	St Resid
6	0,190	0,1000	0,1047	0,0770	-0,0047	-0,17 X

X denotes an observation whose X value gives it large influence.

Durbin-Watson statistic = 2,44741

19. Table of correlations (LEV II – Total Debt to Total Assets)

Correlations: LEV II; TANG; SIZE; GROPP; PROF; VOL; NDTS

	LEV II	TANG	SIZE	GROPP	PROF	VOL
TANG	0,289					
	0,152					
SIZE	0,439	0,412				
	0,025	0,037				
GROPP	-0,641	-0,411	-0,309			
	0,000	0,037	0,125			
PROF	0,281	0,185	0,633	-0,089		
	0,165	0,367	0,001	0,666		
VOL	-0,053	-0,279	-0,404	0,257	-0,479	
	0,798	0,167	0,041	0,205	0,013	
NDTS	-0,319	0,224	-0,114	-0,226	-0,469	-0,190
	0,113	0,272	0,580	0,268	0,016	0,351

Cell Contents: Pearson correlation
             P-Value

20. Historical beta of Schwarz Pharma AG

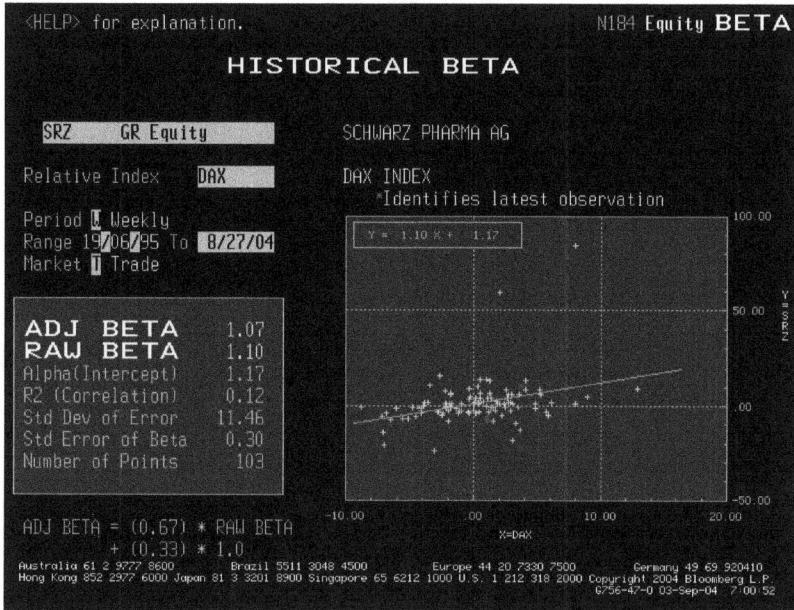

(Source: Bloomberg, 2004)

21. Beta regression model Schwarz Pharma AG versus Dax

Regression Analysis: SWPH versus DAX

The regression equation is
SWPH = 0,0122 + **0,523** DAX

```
Predictor       Coef    SE Coef      T       P
Constant      0,01216   0,01470    0,83    0,410
DAX           0,5231    0,1915     2,73    0,007
```

S = 0,153415   R-Sq = 6,5%   R-Sq(adj) = 5,6%

Analysis of Variance

```
Source           DF       SS        MS       F       P
Regression        1    0,17562   0,17562   7,46   0,007
Residual Error  107    2,51837   0,02354
Total           108    2,69399
```

Durbin-Watson statistic = 1,83142

22. Base country data for Europe and the United States

(Source: Bloomberg, 2004)

Series Subscription

Please enter my subscription to the series *Frankfurter Schriften zu Banking and Finance*, ISSN 1861-096X, as follows:

❏ complete series   OR   ❏ English-language titles
                                                 ❏ German-language titles

starting with
❏ volume # 1
❏ volume # ___
     ❏ please also include the following volumes: #___, ___, ___, ___, ___, ___
❏ the next volume being published;
     ❏ please also include the following volumes: #___, ___, ___, ___, ___, ___

❏ 1 copy per volume   OR   ❏ ___ copies per volume

Subscription within Germany:

You will receive every volume at 1st publication at the regular bookseller's price – incl. s & h and VAT.
Payment:
❏ Please bill me for every volume.
❏ Lastschriftverfahren: Ich/wir ermächtige(n) Sie hiermit widerruflich, den Rechnungsbetrag je Band von meinem/unserem folgendem Konto einzuziehen.

Kontoinhaber: _____ Kreditinstitut: _____
Kontonummer: _____ Bankleitzahl: _____

International Subscription:

Payment (incl. s & h and VAT) in advance for
❏ 10 volumes/copies (€ 319,80)   ❏ 20 volumes/copies (€ 599,80)
❏ 40 volumes/copies (€ 1.099,80)
Please send my books to:

NAME_____ DEPARTMENT_____
ADDRESS _____
POST/ZIP CODE_____ COUNTRY _____
TELEPHONE _____ EMAIL_____

date/signature_____

Please fax to: **0511 / 262 2201 (+49 511 262 2201)**
or mail to: *ibidem*-Verlag, Julius-Leber-Weg 11, D-30457 Hannover, Germany
or send an e-mail: ibidem@ibidem-verlag.de

ibidem-Verlag

Melchiorstr. 15

D-70439 Stuttgart

info@ibidem-verlag.de

www.ibidem-verlag.de
www.edition-noema.de
www.autorenbetreuung.de

www.ingramcontent.com/pod-product-compliance
Lightning Source LLC
Chambersburg PA
CBHW061331220326
41599CB00026B/5131